Big Talk, Small Talk
(and Everything in Between)

Big Talk, Small Talk

Small Talk

(and Everything in Between)

Effective Communication Skills
for All Parts of Your Life

Shola Kaye

Illustrations by Joseph Carrington

ROCKRIDGE
PRESS

Interior and Cover Designer: Eric Pratt
Art Producer: Tom Hood
Editors: Carolyn Abate and Nora Spiegel
Production Manager: Riley Hoffman
Production Editor: Melissa Edeburn
Illustrations © Joseph Carrington, 2020. Author photograph courtesy Marta DeMartini.

ISBN: Print 978-1-64739-058-7 | eBook 978-1-64739-059-4
R0

To Irene. You never said too much or too little, but just enough. And it was always perfect for the occasion.

Introduction

I never considered myself a particularly good communicator. I was more the type to be curled up with a book than interacting with other kids. And as an introvert, I was more of a listener than a talker. At the same time, my grade-school teachers frequently noted that I was friendly but chatted too much in class. What gives?

Years later, after studying the sciences, I found myself spending more time alone in the lab than socializing with friends and family. I came to realize I really needed to brush up on my communication skills, particularly in small-talk situations. I tended to avoid networking events that would have helped me advance my career simply because I wasn't sure what to say to strangers, and I hated the initial awkwardness of walking into a room and not knowing how to approach a group. It always took me a while to warm up. I even avoided chitchat by sitting in the corner and pretending to check my cell phone for an urgent message. On the other hand, I was always the last to leave the event because I eventually hit my stride and enjoyed being in the company of new people.

With the inevitable twists and turns of my career path (something most people today can probably relate to), I was always shifting roles, whether at work or in my personal life. After some time working as a teacher, I went on to become an IT consultant. I then made a dramatic switch and ended up singing professionally for a living. This change meant I had to regularly converse with new clients as well as audience members at parties and other social events. Within the space of a few years, my job morphed from convincing noisy teenagers to settle down to study to encouraging my audiences to forget their woes and get on the dance floor. At the same time, I was moving—New York, Atlanta, London—and each time needing to make new friends.

Now I work as a communication specialist. As a speaking coach, consultant, and keynote speaker, I help individuals, companies, and organizations devise communication strategies or improve their performance at conferences and meetings.

Throughout my journey, I've become increasingly curious about the kinds of skills we need for successful everyday communication, whether it's conversing with followers on social media (as I do as an entrepreneur and small-business owner), calming down an angry friend, or dodging unwanted advances from strangers. Some people are naturally great at communicating and always seem to know the right thing to say. Others have to learn from experience, and that's fine, too. We all have the capacity to be great at interacting. Effective communication is a learnable skill.

Whether you're studying, working, or retired or are single or attached, you can benefit from learning to communicate effectively. This book will give you tools and strategies to clearly and appropriately communicate in everyday face-to-face interactions as well as on social media and messaging apps. You will also walk away with ways to communicate effectively in unique and unpredictable situations.

CHAPTER ONE

Communication Strategies for Life

This chapter explores why it's so important to have good communication skills, and what you can achieve when you can communicate effectively. Some people are lucky enough to develop great communication skills at a young age. Either their parents or mentors teach them these skills, or they just come naturally. But if that's not you, rest assured you can learn these skills, and this book will help.

Vital Life Skills

Human beings are social creatures. From our early days as cave people living in groups, it was necessary to communicate, even if the language we spoke was more akin to guttural utterances and rough gestures than fully formed words. According to a 2012 article in *Psychology Today*, in prehistoric times, humans who weren't able to communicate their value to the group or who irritated those around them likely wouldn't survive for long. Being ostracized would have meant almost certain death. Life would have been short and brutal (or, rather, even shorter and more brutal). Today, the stakes for poor communication aren't quite so high, although we may not always feel that way. Sure, the chances of being singled out and literally eaten by a wild beast are almost nonexistent, but we still need to communicate to thrive and avoid a similar fate, figuratively speaking.

Modern-day languages and communication means are far more sophisticated and plentiful than those available to our prehistoric ancestors. Once we reach adulthood, we're typically not as dependent on our tribe for survival, and we have a bit more latitude and less need to keep the rest of the clan happy. But we can still experience peer pressure, and studies looking at fMRI (functional magnetic resonance imagery), including a 2003 study published by the National Center for Biotechnology Information, show that when we experience rejection, the areas of the brain activated are the same as those activated when we experience physical pain. The best way to avoid this rejection and pain is to know how to interact harmoniously with the people around us. Specifically, we need solid communication skills. Let's explore exactly why communication is so important.

Connection and Empathy

When we communicate with others, the best approach is to establish a connection and demonstrate it with displays of empathy, the ability to understand the feelings of another person. Empathy is vital in getting along with others. If someone is upset or sad, you want to say the appropriate thing to make them feel better, or at least show you understand what they're going through. Can you remember a time when someone put their foot in it by saying something insensitive at the wrong time?

If you can't establish a connection with those around you, and if you struggle to show you belong by failing to understand how others feel, it will be hard for your group to defend you. People will find it difficult to support your ideas and behavior or to stand up for you when times are tough. Empathy is a key skill that makes life easier and relationships richer, and not just with friends, because empathy transcends friendships. Whether you're communicating with a telephone support rep, trying to step into a managerial role at work, or chatting with your kids, empathy and connection will elevate these interactions and you'll become someone people enjoy communicating with.

Credibility and Integrity

Credibility and integrity are critical in our dealings with others. As we establish and develop relationships over time, those around us will be able to measure how much we keep to our word and how consistent we are with our words and deeds. If we want to be seen as a person of integrity, we need to be honest about our intentions, wants, and needs. In some cultures, looking in the eye of a superior or more senior person can be seen as rude or disrespectful, but in Western cultures, good eye contact is typically a sign of honesty and strength. Speaking the truth and looking people in the eye are important, but there's much more to it. Integrity is about being open and consistent, rather than keeping your motivations secret or changing your mind every time the wind blows in a different direction.

To earn credibility, you have to communicate with conviction and be prepared to back up your ideas. If you're a little timid when you communicate, or if you're not used to supporting your statements with body language such as a firm tone and strong eye contact, don't despair. You can work on these behaviors. As you do, be sure to relax. You don't have to be the loudest, most confident person in the room to come across as credible and trustworthy.

Influence and Authority

When we need to make an impact in a situation or display leadership skills, it's useful to convey influence and authority. For example, if we're leading a team or making a decision for the group during an emergency, people are more likely to follow our recommendations if we communicate with some authority.

There's an expression, "Authority isn't given to you—you take it." This isn't to say that you should go argue with your bosses and senior people and try to steal their authority for yourself, but it's important to be mindful of the many ways you can show you are fit to lead and deserve to be taken seriously.

Your tone of voice can show you're someone who commands attention, as can the pace of your words. When we speak quickly, we may come across as nervous or anxious, which takes away from our authority. When we speak firmly with a steady pace, we're more likely to be seen as unflappable and capable. Similarly, jerky body movements or nervous gestures can imply a lack of authority and gravitas, whereas someone who moves fluidly and decisively is often seen as more authoritative. This isn't important only in the workplace. It's also vital in personal relationships with children or a partner. Your tone and body language can make the difference between being disrespected and walked over and being respected and admired.

Your Communication Trail

On any given day, you probably interact with a wide variety of people. We can divide them into three general groups:

Personal relationships. This group may include a significant other, children, parents, siblings, cousins, aunts, uncles, grandparents, and extended family. This group also includes close friends you see or communicate with regularly.

Work relationships. You likely have to deal with coworkers, managers, direct reports, clients, classmates, and associates, regardless of whether you like them. Maybe you send emails or speak on the phone with customers or suppliers. If you work remotely, you might have distant colleagues with whom you communicate by video conference call or email. If you are self-employed or a freelancer, you still have to communicate with clients and colleagues on a regular basis.

Acquaintances and strangers. These are the people you encounter as you go about your day, such as the barista at your local coffee shop and the waitress at the restaurant where you are celebrating your best friend's birthday. It might be the person whose path you cross on the train on the way to work or the guy seated next to you on a plane bound for your next vacation.

Imagine a typical day. You wake up next to your significant other and ask if they slept well, supervise your kids while they eat breakfast, negotiate with your two-year-old to eat the strawberries instead of hurling them across the room, and give some heartfelt encouragement to your oldest daughter, who's a ball of stress anticipating her SAT exam. You jump into the shower, dress, and head to work.

You grab a train ticket at the station, and when your train is delayed, you exchange a few words of commiseration with the woman next to you. You finally get to the office, after picking up a coffee and giving a smile and a nod of recognition to the barista you see at least four times a week. You greet the security guard at the entrance to your office building, exchanging a couple of words about the weather being fantastic for November, before stepping into the elevator. At your desk, you email your colleague at company headquarters, explaining clearly and concisely why you think the company should hire the college grad who interviewed for the intern position yesterday. You then head into a meeting with your boss. Next month is your performance review. You would love to apply for a mortgage and move into that cute new condo complex in your neighborhood, so you're keen for a promotion from associate manager to manager. You take extra care to speak slowly and authoritatively about last month's customer numbers. When your boss gives you the brief for the new project you'll be working on, you show understanding by making strong eye contact, taking notes, and nodding thoughtfully.

At lunch, you pop out to the local diner to meet with a friend who works nearby. Her father has been terminally ill for a number of months, and she's starting to realize she and her siblings are not up to the task of caring for him, but she's having a hard time finding a caregiver she trusts. You show empathy by sharing that you understand her feelings of frustration and exhaustion and by noting how difficult it must be to hold down a full-time job while spending every weekend looking after her dad and searching for a good caregiver.

On the way home, you nearly miss your regular bus, but you wave frantically at the driver and make eye contact, then gesture with open hands in the hope your silent appeal will make her take pity on you. She rolls her eyes but stops the bus. The doors open and you jump in. You catch the eye of the guy standing next to you, and you both smile—you with relief, him with understanding.

WHO DO YOU TALK TO?

Now take a moment to think about *your* average day and your daily interactions.

Where do you go and with whom do you come into contact?

Write down a list of all these people, even if you don't know their names. Some interactions may be in person, others on the phone, and still others by email, text message, social media, or video chat. Any mode of communication counts. Be thorough, and explore the different modes of communication you use and who you're interacting with each time.

Take a moment now to reflect upon these interactions. Where is there room for improvement?

Are there some interactions you look forward to and some you dread? Does anything stand out as an ideal conversation or interaction? Was anything particularly challenging? Are there areas of interaction you'd like to improve upon?

Keep this list handy while you read this book. As you learn new communication strategies, think about how you can apply them to these interactions. Set a goal for improving these communications, especially the challenging and dreaded ones. For example, you may dislike talking to one of your colleagues. Think carefully about why this is. You might even choose a handful of people you find difficult and take on the challenge of using this book to improve those communications. There might not be an immediate benefit beyond your personal growth, but some unexpected advantages may arise. You may find a way to befriend someone who formerly irritated you, or build a better relationship with a troublesome client. You may even grow to like (or at least find peace with) your mother-in-law or another relative with whom you've been feuding for years. If you develop a positive or even neutral expectation instead of anticipating the same old communication struggles, all kinds of opportunities might await you.

The Ways We Communicate

Now that we've considered who we talk to, let's explore the tools we have to help us convey information clearly and expressively. Verbal communication is more than just the words we use; it's also the way we use them. We can think of the words as the meat (or if you're veggie or vegan, the main), whereas our other vehicles of communication are the sides and the seasoning. These include tone, gestures, and facial expressions. As we've touched on, even the pace at which we speak can have repercussions on how other people receive our message.

Then, of course, we have the written word. Some people are skilled at adding subtle meaning to their words on paper or in text form, but most of us need to tread carefully when writing because people can't use our gestures, tone, and expressions to confirm whether they should interpret our message as friendly, warm, or something else.

This book covers casual chitchat, important conversation, nonverbal communication, and written communication. No matter how you need to get your point across, this book provides tips to help you carry yourself successfully through most interpersonal exchanges.

Without Words

When we speak, we have so many choices about how we deliver our message. As a communication coach, I often work with clients to improve their public-speaking skills. I see people working hard on their presentation slides and the words they plan to say. What they don't rehearse, but is just as important, is their delivery. This includes whether they stand up straight or slouch, whether they look people in the eye or gaze at the ground, and whether their gestures are relaxed and natural or practiced or robotic. Do their hands hang awkwardly by their sides or visibly tremble while clutching a piece of paper? An audience can quickly pick up on whether the speaker is happy or reluctant to be standing before them, whether they fully believe in their message or are ambivalent, and so much more. Nonverbal cues are incredibly important because they send their own message completely independent of the words being spoken.

Of course, our nonverbal expression isn't just related to public speaking. In fact, a prepared presentation can be a little easier because we get the chance to rehearse, so we can deliver our content without interruption. In our spontaneous day-to-day interactions, we can get caught by surprise or be blindsided by information we hadn't bargained on, such as finding out a supplier has just gone out of business or being interrupted by an impatient colleague. Unexpected events can distract or upset us, resulting in a flustered response.

FACIAL CUES

You take a break and go to a bakery to pick up a pastry. The young woman who attends to you is polite, taking your order and saying thank-you, but she looks as though she's about to cry. Her mouth is turned down at the ends, her eyes are filled with tears, and she's reluctant to look you in the eye. Instead of smiling cheerfully and saying a few words about looking forward to your croissant (which smells delicious), you look at the woman sympathetically with warm eyes and an expression that says, "I hope everything works out okay."

BODY LANGUAGE

Your best buddy, whom you've known for years, is the expressive type. Typically, he greets you with a huge smile and a bear hug. Today, however, as you greet each other in the restaurant, you can sense tension in his body. He looks distracted, and as you step toward him for your usual hug, he shakes his head slightly with eyes downcast. His hands are clenched into fists and his eyes look past you. You don't sense any hostility toward you, but something is definitely wrong. You mentally prepare yourself to hear bad news, listen attentively, and provide as much support as you can.

POSTURES (SEATED AND STANDING)

At the office, your excellent work is getting noticed and you've been asked to run a meeting with a different department to brief them on some upcoming process changes. You're new to your role and want to make a good impression. You know the importance of maintaining good posture to convey authority, gravitas, and confidence so everyone in the meeting will get the sense that you know your subject and your ideas are worth listening to.

Although you feel a bit nervous, you walk into the room with your head held high, shoulders down (not hunched), and back straight. As you sit down to run the meeting, you continue with your erect posture, conveying to others that you're alert and tuned in. When others speak, you lean in a bit so everyone can see that you're listening and interested.

GESTURES

Your teenage daughter is bringing home her new girlfriend to dinner for the first time. You can tell they both feel a little nervous about the event, and you want your daughter's date to feel welcome without feeling overwhelmed. As you open the front door, you smile and extend your arms as if to say, "Come on in, you're very welcome here." As she walks through the door, you keep your body language open and friendly, gesturing toward your husband and son as you introduce them. You then reach out for her jacket and give a friendly nod as she removes it and hands it to you. You point out the living room with a relaxed look in that direction and invite her to go on in.

Verbally

We often see verbal expression as the cornerstone of human communication, but verbal communication is so much more than words. It's word choice and, of course, tone of voice. Changing our tone of voice can alter or even reverse the meaning of our words, even if we say the exact same sentence.

Consider this sentence: "I love you." Seems straightforward enough, right? But let's look a little closer:

I love you: The emphasis on the **"I"** means *I* love you but perhaps someone else doesn't.

I *love* you: The emphasis on **"love"** implies the emotion being felt is in question and the speaker is making it clear that it's love.

I love *you*: The emphasis on the **"you"** means I love *you* and not someone else.

Active listening involves more than just hearing a string of words and ascribing meaning. It involves layering this basic meaning with the more challenging task of listening for tone and emphasis to get the speaker's true meaning.

SPEAKING

Let's continue to play around with the "I love you" sentence. We could say "I love you" in an inquisitive tone. "I love *you*?" sounds like a woman has recently come out of a coma and just been told the person in front of her is her fiancé, but she's not so sure. It sounds indecisive.

Let's take it to the workplace with a different sentence: "I want this job." Imagine there's an opening available and you need to convince your boss you deserve a promotion. You might say:

"I *want* this job." This expression is **declarative**. You're declaring this is the job for you.

"*I* want this job." This comes across as **determined**, like you are throwing yourself into the competitive arena and ready to take on anyone to get the job you desire.

"I want *this* job?" Now you don't sound so sure; in fact, you seem a bit **indecisive**.

Word choice is also a factor. Two people might enjoy the same meal equally, but one will describe it as "fantastic" and the other might characterize it as "not bad." Of course, there may be situations in which you carefully choose whether to overstate, state, or understate. If a friend was sick and couldn't join you for dinner, you wouldn't want to gush about what a "fantastic" meal you had without her. "Not bad" might be the more empathetic answer. If your friend invited you to dine as her guest, however, "fantastic" might be the more appropriate response when she asks what you thought of the meal.

Another factor is the level of sophistication in someone's language. Contrast "Would you kindly tell me the location of the shoe department?" with "Where are the shoes?" The amount of sophistication you use might depend on cultural expectations, what you're accustomed to, with whom you're speaking, or whether you're trying to make a particular impression. It also depends on whether you're writing or speaking, and what medium you're using. For example, if you're writing a message on Twitter, you'll need to #keepitbrief.

ACTIVE LISTENING

This skill goes hand-in-hand with speaking. If we fail to listen actively, we'll lose much of the meaning of the words being spoken. Active listening involves being present to the speaker and minimizing the thoughts going on in our heads. The best listeners pay attention and try to understand rather than think about what they want to say next. Active listening assesses the speaker's message, tone, and word choice to get a rounded picture of who we're talking to, their state of mind, and what they are trying to convey. It's not easy when there's so much competition for our attention, but we can do it, and it reaps rewards. Everyone loves a good listener.

Written Words

Texting, email, and social media are just some of the ways we communicate with each other in writing. However, the old-school methods, such as putting pen to paper for notes, letters, and greeting cards, still have their charm. If those options seem too trivial and you have a big message to share, you can certainly ask for your beloved's hand in marriage with a proposal on a jumbotron at the football game, or share your company's advertising message on a billboard.

Mark Twain famously said, "I didn't have the time to write a short letter, so I wrote a long one instead." Sometimes it takes much more effort to craft a brief message because we have to be extra selective about our choice of words. Did you ever receive a text message that made you raise your eyebrows because the tone seemed negative or off-color? Maybe that wasn't the writer's intention, but it can be difficult to convey complex concepts and emotions in short bodies of text. Emojis can help convey an intended tone in some casual situations, but they're not always appropriate, particularly in a profes-sional, academic, or work environment. If something strikes you as negative or offensive, it pays to consider carefully before shooting off an angry email response or posting a very public Facebook comment about something that makes your blood boil. People have been fired from their jobs for less.

Take a little extra time to craft any public message that might convey or arouse emotion in the people who read it. Likewise, if you're feeling upset and want to fire off a brusque message to a friend, consider picking up the phone instead. Putting things in writing memorializes them forever. Con-versely, an in-person or phone conversation might save time and help you quickly resolve the issue, rather than provoking a string of back-and-forth messages that prolong the dispute and distract you for hours.

Visual Aids

We typically use visual aids at work more than at home. A teacher may use a model of the gut during biology class to help students understand digestion. A freelance graphic designer pitching for new business might prepare a storyboard to show off her work. A crossing guard helping kids across the street before and after school employs hand signals or a sign to warn approaching vehicles to stop and beckon the children to cross the road.

There are, however, messages to pick up in the nonwork environment, too. For example, if you're a salesperson visiting a home where you see shoes piled up in the hallway and residents padding around in slippers or socks, that's a pretty strong indication you'll be required to take off your footwear before entering.

A couple of days ago, I was driving down a narrow street with cars on both sides and saw a double-parked car when, just a few feet away, there was a parking space they could have used. The message I took away was that the person was in a hurry, and perhaps a little inconsiderate.

When I'm trying to follow a healthy eating regimen I sometimes leave neon-colored sticky notes on the refrigerator with written reminders of what I should eat that day.

A friend who works from home installed a red light outside his office door. When the light is on, it signals his young sons that Daddy is busy and mustn't be disturbed. When it's off, the kids are welcome to come in. A less sophisticated but equally telling version of this might be the sign a teenager posts on her bedroom door warning parents and siblings to "Stay out or else!"

About This Book

As you probably guessed from the title, in this book we cover three different communication themes: big talk, small talk, and everything in between. "Everything in between" encompasses nonverbal, written, and visual communications. I've grouped it this way so you can easily reference ideas relating to the different situations you find yourself in.

If you haven't already completed the exercise in the section "Who Do You Talk To?" (page 8), I encourage you to circle back and tackle it before moving through the next chapters, as it will guide you toward the scenarios that best match your daily interactions. Think about where you need the most guidance. Are you a whiz at small talk and networking at parties, but you get stressed every time you have to have a heart-to-heart with your partner? Do you spend hours each day texting with your friends, but when you have to pick up the phone to wish your gramps a happy birthday, you put it off until the last possible moment because you find it awkward?

This book brings everything together in an organized set of stories and strategies that reflect everyday life, so you can master all the communications that matter to you, whether it's having intimate talks with your partner or figuring out what to say to a coworker to open the lines of communication for a more rewarding relationship.

Small Talk

Some people struggle a bit with small talk and prefer to dive straight into the big topics. But small talk is a great way to build up a bit of empathy and find things you have in common, which can provide the groundwork for creating a deeper relationship.

Chapter 2 explores ways to elevate your small talk as it relates to meeting new people at work events, chatting with others on vacation or at parties and social gatherings, and even engaging in conversation with an elderly neighbor. Random conversations with the barista, bartender, or cashier can be fun and enriching interactions. The student who serves you coffee and comments casually that they're looking for an internship at a tech company might be a great candidate for one of your clients. That elderly neighbor might have great taste in books, gardening, or music, sparking a rewarding dialogue or potential friendship.

Big Talk

Negotiations, disagreements, and important matters are an inevitable part of life. If we don't manage these matters in a timely way, they can come back to bite us or careen out of control. Many of us prefer to keep it light and positive, but sometimes we have to get serious, and that's where this chapter will help. Chapter 3 provides strategies for effectively navigating these important or difficult conversations. Perhaps you need to make a big impression during a job interview, function, meeting, or presentation. Or maybe you're thinking about ending a relationship and need to have a serious talk to see if you might be able to effect change in your partner's behavior. Perhaps you have sibling issues and it's time to wipe the slate clean.

I recently had a three-way conversation with my siblings as we debated how to care for our elderly parents, who refuse to leave a too-large house that they're struggling to look after. Whatever big issues you may encounter, you'll learn to handle their accompanying big talk with grace and a level head.

Everything in Between

Aside from big and small talk, we have countless daily interactions that don't involve conversation. These interactions could take the form of a raised eyebrow in response to your boss's suggestion that the deadline be moved from next week to tomorrow, a gentle, encouraging pat on your child's shoulder as they do their homework, or a quick text reminder for your partner to pick up the groceries before heading home from basketball practice.

NONVERBAL CUES

There are many ways we can behave thoughtfully without speaking. You get up from your seat on the bus to allow a pregnant woman to sit down. In the line at the grocery store, you allow the man behind you to take your spot because he has only two items and you have a full shopping cart. Your niece has a dental appointment and you purchase her a new book from her favorite author to give her something distracting to read.

WRITTEN AND VISUAL AIDS

Solid written and visual skills involve choosing the right medium for the message you'd like to convey, whether it's personal, social, or work-related. Examples include such things as:

- A quick good-luck text to a colleague who's interviewing for a promotion at work

- A message of thanks on Facebook after your friends call and message you with birthday wishes

- A "Do Not Disturb" sign on your bedroom door to remind the kids not to wake their mom first thing in the morning after she worked late the night before

- A sticky note on the lunch bag you packed for your partner

- A video congratulating your distant relative on their graduation

- A chart or slideshow for a presentation

It's important to consider which medium best fits the scenario. A handwritten note is a more fitting response than a text to the person who hosted a surprise party in your honor. And Grandma would like a phone call when the baby's born—by announcing the birth only on Facebook, you miss her awesome reaction (and risk hurting her feelings)!

Chapter Details

The content within each chapter is broken down into different types of scenarios centered around the three key areas of life: personal relationships, work relationships, and interactions with acquaintances and strangers. For each area, I provide verbal and nonverbal strategies, along with sample dialogue, to show you how you might approach a particular situation using effective communication skills. All the strategies are based on real experiences, but I've changed the names and identifying characteristics.

You might find certain areas challenging. Perhaps you hate talking on the phone and prefer to text, or you feel awkward engaging in small talk but want to improve. Take heart. If you use these strategies, or read the ones in this book and create your own, you *will* improve. You can even practice one or two strategies per week as often as you can. I've seen clients have so much success with these methods. One client who works in real estate used these strategies and frameworks and contacted me excitedly just days later, saying "They worked!"

So let's make them work for you!

○ ○ ○

CHAPTER TWO

Engaging Small Talk

Small talk is underrated. You may hate idle chitchat, but the reality is that it helps people relax and understand that they're talking to a potential friend rather than a foe. Don't be afraid to talk about the day-to-day things in life, such as friends and family, work, recreation, and anecdotes from your past. Here, you'll find some common scenarios in which you might need to make small talk at work, socially, or with complete strangers.

It's Okay to Talk to Strangers (Especially When You're Networking)

Business networking can prove tricky for some people, but it doesn't have to be. A gentle, more sociable approach can be more effective than aggressively thrusting your business card into as many hands as possible.

You've just packed up your belongings and moved to a different city to start a new job. You're keen to make some new professional contacts, so you register to attend a monthly networking event for individuals in the legal profession. You like the description of the event, which sounds high-energy, focused, and with a good mix of legal practitioners and those who serve the legal industry. It seems to attract good numbers, and the blurb on the invite makes the attendees sound like a friendly bunch worth getting to know.

Traffic is terrible, so you arrive a little later than you'd hoped. By the time you walk through the door, the event is in full swing. People are laughing, and everyone seems to know everyone else. They're standing in groups of different sizes clutching glasses of beer or red wine.

You gulp, feeling a bit intimidated and wanting to turn around and flee, but then you mentally shake it off and proceed into the room. You visit the bar to collect a glass of wine, then look around to decide which group to approach. You decide on a large group of four or five people. It's large enough that they're probably not discussing anything private. You walk up and stand in one of the gaps between people, catch the eye of the man next to you, and smile brightly. "I'm new to this event. Do you mind if I join you?"

The woman who was animatedly speaking to the small group pauses, and the guy next to you smiles and shuffles to the side a little to let you in. *Phew,* you think. *It wasn't that hard.*

It's noisy, and the group is now growing a little too large for everyone to continue to follow the speaker's story, so your neighbor turns to you and asks what brings you here. The two of you launch into a lighthearted conversation about the networking group. Although you're there for work, you keep the conversation fun and friendly. When he reveals he plays tennis, you ask where he plays and chat about nonwork topics to establish a rapport. You keep your tone warm and open, smiling and nodding to encourage him to continue. To keep the conversation going, you comment about playing tennis in your old city and looking for courts in your new town. Your conversation partner volunteers a few suggestions, which you note with thanks.

Once you've established a rapport with this small talk, you eventually move on to topics of work and share that you are looking to meet more young professionals. It turns out that your new friend is an avid networker. He rattles off several events you might like and offers to email them to you the next day. You exchange business cards, making a mental note to jot on the card who he is and what you talked about. You thank him warmly and tell him you look forward to keeping in touch. You walk away, smiling and more relaxed now that you have some tips to help you socially and with work. It was a productive conversation—and good networking practice.

> **TIP**
>
> At networking events, it's helpful to keep things light and establish a rapport with small talk before diving into work-related matters. People tend to open up more once they feel they're talking to a friend, not someone who's mining them for information. Seek to make a genuine connection and you'll do fine.

Sparkle to Spark up a Conversation

What's a handy and effective way to warm someone up and kick off a conversation? Paying a compliment or making a thoughtful observation are terrific options.

Imagine yourself at a social event with a bunch of strangers. Your friend brought you along as his wingwoman, and you're not enjoying that *I-don't-know-anyone-here* feeling. You glance at the woman next to you, who is wearing an electric blue jacket with unusually shaped lapels. It's clear from the eye-popping color and unique tailoring that she took time and effort to put together her outfit.

You approach with a simple hello and say, "I really do love the little notches on the lapels of your jacket. I've never seen anything like them before. My dad was a tailor. The workmanship on your blazer is super detailed. Was it tailored for you?" The key with this compliment is that it's quite specific and tied to a short personal story. You're revealing a very real interest in the feature you've highlighted, which shows sincerity.

It's easy to make compliments like, "Wow, love the color of that bag," or "You hair looks nice," but they don't necessarily deepen the conversation. Sometimes we are reluctant to compliment another person in case they take it the wrong way. If you are specific and focus on something that is a little unusual, the compliment is more likely to be well-received.

You can actually use this as a strategy for yourself. Wear an unusual scarf, a bright color, or something else that catches the eye. The item doesn't have to be new, expensive, or one-of-a-kind. You might carry a notebook with an unusual design or select a unique cell phone cover. Anything out of the ordinary and chosen with care will invite conversation from the people around you and can make it easier to get talking. Contrast these two responses:

Someone says, "Wow, what a cool cell phone cover. I love that it's in the shape of a baseball. You'd never lose that in your bag." You could simply reply, "Oh thanks." Or, you could say, "Thanks, I love it, too. I'm a baseball fanatic, and when I lived in Nashville, I played every week for fun. Now that I've moved to Brooklyn I rarely play, so this phone cover reminds me of how much I love the game."

The second example gives the other person plenty of conversational hooks. The conversation could go in so many directions, such as a discussion of baseball, Nashville, Brooklyn, moving to another state, or even more chatter about the variety of phone covers available.

TIP

Compliments make great icebreakers. If you choose to carry an eye-catching item, make sure you're ready with a few follow-up comments to keep the conversation going.

Put Them at Ease with a Story

Telling stories is a handy way to defuse tension and make everyone feel more relaxed.

Your 8-year-old son has invited his best friend, Corey, over for dinner, and it's clear that Corey is nervous. He's watching your every move with wide, panicked eyes and seems too afraid to pick up his fork to eat.

When his mom dropped him off, she warned you that Corey can be timid. She confided that although he loves hanging out with your son, Mike, he almost refused the invitation because he was afraid to meet the rest of Mike's family.

"Hey, Corey," you ask gently, "is this the first time you've had dinner at a friend's home?" Corey nods slowly and silently, his eyes like saucers and his lips scrunched together as though afraid to speak. You think about how to put Corey at ease, and try to dredge up some memories of hanging out with friends when you were a kid.

"It can be scary going to someone else's house. Even though you want to spend time with your friend, it's hard to meet the whole family, too, right?"

You decide to tell the kids a semi-embarrassing story of one of your childhood faux pas and hope it will help Corey loosen up and enjoy the evening. You start by setting the scene, including your perspective at the time.

"I remember the first time I had dinner with my best friend, Sam. We were super close friends, but she had three big brothers who seemed like giants to me, plus two dogs. I was an only child, so her house seemed loud and crazy. One day I went over there for dinner. I was trying not to be scared of the dogs and the brothers and Sam's very friendly but very loud dad. I tried to just focus on eating my burger. The next thing

I knew, one of the dogs jumped up at me and gave me such a fright that I knocked over my glass of water. It spilled right into her dad's lap!

"He was completely soaked. I started to cry. I was embarrassed and so afraid that I'd never be able to play with Sam again. But her dad just laughed and said, 'Hey, don't worry. In a crazy house like this, accidents happen all the time!' And he went upstairs and got changed.

"Sam's dad was so sweet and kind. Even though I made a complete fool of myself, it was almost like nothing had happened. He just laughed about it, and we carried on joking about it for a long time after that.

"So, Corey, I'm pretty sure you're not going to spill water over the table. But even if you did, it wouldn't matter. You're sitting next to Mike, not me, so if you do spill anything, he's the one who will have to change!" By the time you get to the end of your story, Corey is smiling and laughing as he pictures you scared out of your wits and Sam's dad soaking wet. Corey manages to eat half of his spaghetti, and the two boys run off and play. Before Corey leaves, you tell him, "You're very welcome here. Come over whenever you feel like it. I'm so proud Mike has a friend like you."

TIP

Brush up on your conversation game by thinking up a few short stories, such as moments you tried something for the first time or times you experienced an epic fail. Used judiciously, these stories can be great for putting people at ease and helping you come across as an amusing and interesting conversationalist.

Remember Who You're Talking to—Names Are Important

It's nice when you remember the name of someone you just met at a social event, although it's not always easy to do so.

You're at a fundraising mixer for the parents of your kid's soccer team. Your daughter is new to the team, so you don't know many of the parents. As you mingle with the group, you wonder how you're going to keep so many names straight. There's Doug, and Janelle, and Mark, or is it Martin? Uh-oh, you're already forgetting some of the names. At that moment Doug (or is it Dave?) approaches and asks if you'd like a beer. You smile and nod thanks without using his name. You're concerned because you know some people can be offended if you get their name wrong, and you don't want to ruffle any feathers or appear careless.

Then you recall that using someone's name as much as you can in the first few seconds can help keep it top of mind, and that making associations can also help. You decide to start the evening fresh. You'll admit you're not so great with names but will strive to do better by using these two tactics.

As Dave/Doug approaches with your beer, you smile warmly and say, "Thank you so much. I'm so sorry, did you say your name is Dave?"

"Nope, it's Doug," he responds.

"I'm awful with names, Doug. I hope you can forgive me. Does anyone ever call you Douglas? My mom would only ever call me by my full name when I was in trouble." Mentally, you make some associations connected to the word Doug. Hmmm, Doug—I *dug* a hole for myself when I didn't remember his name. Doug E. Fresh the rapper and Michael Douglas the actor. All this takes just a split second, but it helps you cement Doug's name in your mind.

When you get names wrong or aren't quite sure what to call the person, another approach is to joke about predictive text names. I frequently see my name spelled as "Shops" in text messaging because not many people have Shola programmed as a word into their phone. This could be a fun topic of conversation. Ask your conversation partner, "When have you really messed up someone's name while texting?" This will ease any tension and get them to see you're well-meaning—and their response might even reveal their name!

> **TIP**
>
> When you meet someone new, make an effort to remember their name immediately. Make an association or use it frequently until it becomes embedded in your memory. If you're not great at names, work to get better, and keep on hand an amusing story or a go-to comment to help lighten up the situation.

When to Be Careful with Compliments: What You Don't Say Counts

Have you ever been in a situation where someone complimented you for a job well done but ignored everyone else's efforts? You probably felt a little embarrassed and awkward because you were being singled out, and maybe even concerned that the attention made others resentful. Here's an example:

You and two colleagues are making presentations to your team. You have put in the preparation time, done your homework, and made sure your message, slides, and talking points are top-notch. Your coworkers Briona and Stan, however, have been busy with other projects and haven't had as much time to prepare. In fact, Briona asked your team lead, Layla, a couple of days before the meeting if she could present her talk next month instead. Layla refused and said, "Just do your best. I know you'll be fine."

The day of the meeting, Briona and Stan go first. Their presentations are not great, but they get the basic information across. Your own presentation is clearly a cut above. Your graphics and slides are polished. You've had plenty of time to rehearse exactly what you want to say, and your transitions are smooth. The hours you've spent preparing in front of the mirror pay off, and you receive an ovation from the team. Layla is glowing with praise. She announces in front of the team of 20, "That was one of the best presentations I've ever seen. I absolutely loved it. You did a fantastic job and set a great example. It was head and shoulders above the other talks we've seen today, and I want to commend you on your hard work."

You smile with pride but also feel a sting of embarrassment because you clearly had much more time than the others to prepare, and yet Layla didn't mention that to the group. As she continues to praise you, Briona and Stan look down and sink into their seats. Clearly the lack of acknowledgment for their efforts and the heaping praise for yours has made them feel embarrassed and dejected.

Layla finishes off by saying, "I hope you all took note of how great that presentation was. Let this be the new standard for the team. Don't come to me with anything less—let's set the bar higher." You smile thinly but also feel very awkward that no one has acknowledged that you didn't have a level playing field. At the end of the presentation, Briona and Stan don't look at you, and they are first to leave the room.

It seems everyone is left feeling bad—except perhaps Layla. What would you have done differently if you were Layla? Might you have toned down your generous praise and shared your feedback with each team member in private, rather than shaming the weaker presenters in front of the group? Could you also have shared your opinion on each presentation but acknowledged that Stan and Briona did a commendable job considering the short amount of time they had to prepare? Can you think of other ways you might have communicated more thoughtfully than Layla?

TIP

If you're singling someone out for a compliment, make sure you're aware of the impact on others within earshot. Take care not to unwittingly play people off against each other or inadvertently insult or slight one person while praising another.

Keep Your Communication Consistent

You're on a first date with Liam, whom you recently met online. All his communications have been open, friendly, and kind. You exchanged some great messages before you met, and you had a few relaxed phone conversations, during which you both shared goals, aspirations, and details about your lives.

Now you are meeting for the first time, and things are going well. You're at a fun Italian restaurant with a hip, bubbly atmosphere. Music plays in the background and the waitstaff buzz about in a friendly, efficient manner. So far, the service has been impeccable. The food is well seasoned and enjoyable. You've looked forward to this date all week and expected to have a great time.

And yet, each time the waiter approaches Liam to ask him what he'd like, your date's tone changes. He becomes very curt, almost rude, and doesn't even look the waiter in the eye. He scowls and rattles off instructions about the wine, barking out his choices in a way you find unacceptable.

The waiter, a young man barely out of his teens, blushes slightly, his friendly smile faltering as Liam continues with his bossy and imperious behavior. You can't believe you're out with someone who treats the server like this. You remember when you served customers like Liam while you were waiting tables in college, and you don't feel good about the date. What a jerk.

To compensate for Liam's rudeness, you make extra strong eye contact with the waiter each time he comes over, nodding and smiling as you share your choices from the menu and thanking him each time. You finally decide to ask Liam if there's a problem. "Hey, what do you think of our waiter? He seems really nice and attentive."

Liam shrugs. "Who cares about the waitstaff? The less I see of them, the better. These kids tend not to know what they're doing—most of them are lousy at their jobs."

Whoa, you think. *I'm not so sure I like this guy.* You begin to reassess your initial opinion of Liam and decide to monitor him a little more closely. You respond, "I think he's doing really well. I worked in a bar for years while I was at college, and I detested the patrons who acted like they were better than us. You have to expect a few like that, but fortunately most of them were polite and friendly. I've even stayed in touch with one or two to this day." You are curious about how Liam will respond.

"That's all well and good," he says, "but I have more important things to think about than how I treat the staff. I'm here spending my money. That should be enough."

Yikes, you think. *This might turn out to be a long evening, and not one to be repeated.*

> **TIP**
>
> How we communicate with others is a strong indicator of who we really are. People pick up on the disparities between how we treat them and how we treat others, particularly those who can't fight back. Treat everyone with warmth and courtesy, regardless of whether you need to impress them.

Don't Indulge the Naysayers

Although it can be tempting to speak negatively about a situation, it usually pays to take the conversational high road.

You're at the train station on a packed platform at 8 a.m., about to catch your ride to an important kickoff meeting with a new client. The train is already delayed 10 minutes when a message flashes that it has been canceled and the next one won't arrive for another 30 minutes.

You groan inwardly and text your client that you'll be late. You hope she will overlook it, as this is not the kind of impression you want to make, especially at a first meeting.

The guy next to you curses loudly. He had been stomping around in the confined space on the platform, agitated and muttering, clearly impatient for the train to arrive. The cancellation seems to have pushed him over the edge. He catches your eye and launches into an attack on the train company. "I cannot believe these fools! This service is absolutely [expletive] horrendous. I can't believe I pay thousands of dollars a year on rail tickets only to be jerked around every day. What are these idiots doing? They should have the franchise taken away from them." He looks at you expectantly, waiting for you to join in the diatribe and weigh in with your own string of curses and display of frustration.

You feel his pain and are just as irritated by the poor service, but you decide that a busy train platform is not the time and place for a scene. It's the beginning of the day and you know if you allow yourself to slide down the slippery slope of negativity, your mood will only worsen. Plus, you'd rather not be known among your fellow commuters, many of whom you see daily, for being a grumbler. You pride yourself on exercising self-control and choosing your words wisely.

You finally respond, "I agree it's frustrating. I'm a freelancer and I have a client meeting I need to get to. But things could be far worse. During that snowstorm last year, we didn't have trains for four days and I lost some business."

The guy gives you a penetrating look. You can see he's deciding whether to keep chatting or find a richer seam of negativity elsewhere. With a shrug, he decides that complaining to you is not producing the desired reaction. He purses his lips and steps away, and you hear him berating a representative from the train company. *Better them than me*, you think, happy to have averted the situation. You put on your headphones and decide to soothe yourself with a song by your favorite band while you wait for the next train.

> **TIP**
>
> Negativity is contagious, and it can spiral out of control, so choose your moments to complain wisely—and preferably not in public, unless you feel you have a strong cause. Acknowledge the situation, but try to make a positive or neutral remark to steer the conversation in the right direction.

How to Talk to a Stranger Who Might Need Help

Don't be afraid to lend a hand to a person in need, even though it might feel a little awkward.

You're walking back from the grocery store on a Saturday afternoon, thinking about the delicious fish stew you're going to cook when you get home. As you cross the street, you notice an older woman getting off a bus. She appears to be struggling. The bus has already driven away, but the woman has fallen onto the sidewalk. She's alone and no one else is close by. You want to rush over and check that she's okay. But what do you say?

When in doubt, help out. In this situation, express your concern and relay that you're there to help by saying something like, "I saw you fall—are you okay?" Sometimes the person will be happy to get assistance and will grab your hand. Other times, the person will feel embarrassed or want to avoid a fuss and will quickly brush off your attempt to help. But offer support even if the other person might not welcome it.

Even if the woman says she's okay and can get up by herself, wait around for a few minutes to ensure she's steady on her feet and able to get home. You can ask questions like, "Do you have far to walk?" or "Can I walk with you to where you're going?" or "Is there anyone we can call?" If she's truly sick and needs a doctor or an ambulance, you can call medical services and stay with her until they arrive. In this case, you can keep some light conversation going without being too intrusive. You might not want to ask her what's wrong, or if this has happened before. This incident may be related to an ongoing medical condition she doesn't want to share. Instead, you can display empathy, saying something like, "Gosh, the buses move on so quickly these days, don't they?" or "My neighbor tripped a few days ago and suffered a bruised knee, but he's back to normal."

Your role is to be concerned and kind but respectful of her privacy, unless she decides she wants to share. If this is the case, you can be empathetic, but it's okay to steer the conversation toward small talk if her candor makes you uncomfortable.

Psychologists have found an unfortunate bias that people have against responding to people in need, as we tend to assume that someone else is closer, better able to help, or more qualified to lend a hand. Although it's human behavior to hang back to see what others will do first, push yourself to be the leader. Don't wait for someone else to make the first move.

TIP

When you see someone in distress and are concerned for their well-being, you can simply ask if they're okay. Don't wait for someone else to take the lead. It's better to ask and have them wave you away than ignore them only to feel regretful later that you could have made a difference. Sometimes just a few words of sympathy can make a tremendous impact.

Get What You Pay For (But Go Easy on the Staff)

When you feel a company or store is treating you poorly, you may be tempted to take it out on a staff member, but try to stay cool.

You were eyeing a pair of pants to wear to your best friend's party and finally decided to take the plunge and buy them. They weren't cheap, but they had a classic cut and were made by a decent brand, so you figured they'd be a good investment and would last a few years. But after wearing the pants just once, dancing the night away, you discover the side seam has come undone and your skin was exposed. You hope no one saw it.

You take the pants back to the store. They should have been more durable, and you're frustrated that the quality was so low given the high price you paid. Unfortunately, it's been more than 30 days since you bought the garment, and the store policy does not guarantee refunds after this point. You approach the customer service desk feeling irritated that you have to make a case, but you remember to be polite and courteous. After all, the young guy behind the counter didn't make the pants. It wasn't his fault.

"Excuse me," you say. "I bought these pants here, but can you see how this seam is ripped?" The guy examines the pants and the receipt. "Oh, you bought them more than 30 days ago," he says. "Let me check if we can still give you a refund."

Although you want to snap that he sure as heck had better be in a position to get your money back, you hold your tongue. After all, it pays to be polite—firm and no-nonsense, but not hysterical. The clerk returns and explains, "Sorry, but the refund period has expired, so there's nothing we can do." You decide to escalate the situation rather than arguing. You hate scenes and your heart is pounding, but you need to take this further. You take a deep breath, and in the same assertive tone, you say, "Can you kindly get the manager? The seam was clearly poorly stitched. The item was faulty. I wore these pants only once, and I need to talk to someone who is authorized to help me."

Within a couple of minutes, the store manager is in front of you. You state firmly but unemotionally that you are a good customer, the pants were faulty, and you are firm on seeking a fair solution. The manager offers to let you exchange them for an item up to the same value. You are happy that your strategy to stay resolute and not accept no for an answer has served you well, and proud you were able to resolve your issue calmly.

> **TIP**
>
> When making a complaint in a store, it doesn't pay to fly off the handle. The most effective response is to stay cool and in control. You can make it clear from your words, tone of voice, and body language that you're not going to be brushed off with an unsatisfactory response.

Small Talk Can Lead to Big Opportunities

Small talk gets a bad rap because some people see it as trivial or inconsequential. But sometimes small talk can pay off big. From a friend who works in sales, I learned a great little framework you can use to come up with topics for small talk. It's called FORM, for Family, Occupation, Recreation, and Motivation. All these topics are lighthearted and inoffensive, but they can lead to deeper conversation and beneficial opportunities. As any salesperson will tell you, opportunities come out of conversations. Think about it from a buyer's perspective. Would you be more comfortable making a purchase from someone with whom you've had a relaxed conversation or a complete stranger with whom you've barely exchanged a word? This is not to say that you should see every chance conversation as an opportunity to find a new partner or learn about a new financial opportunity, but you never know!

My partner, George, loves to ask questions, which is a good strategy when making small talk, because people usually love to chat about themselves. He recently decided to sell an old coffee maker on eBay. The highest bidder was a young guy. He came over on a Saturday morning to pick up the machine. Most people would have opened the door, handed over the coffee maker with a smile, and bid the buyer farewell, but not George. He invited the buyer into the kitchen, found out his name (Stephan), and offered him a full demo of the machine so he could sample the coffee.

George then asked Stephan a series of questions beginning with, "What made you want to buy the machine?" Stephan replied that he loved a good coffee and that his dad owned a similar machine.

That simple question evolved into a conversation in which we learned Stephan had just started a new job in London and was working in the same industry as George. It turned out George knew of the company where Stephan worked and was interested in the project Stephan was involved with. After another few more minutes of animated conversation, the meeting ended with the two men connecting on LinkedIn and making plans to get a drink after work. All this from a simple, open-ended question about the motivation to buy a coffee machine.

Don't be afraid to find out a little about the stranger sitting next to you at the diner where you're enjoying a quick coffee before picking up your kid from soccer practice. You never know what could come from it. If you don't enjoy small talk, after a few warm-up questions you might want to go straight for the motivation questions. "Why" questions can seem a bit intrusive at first, so start out with some closed-answer questions such as "What kind of coffee are you drinking?" or "Are you local to this neighborhood?" The conversation that results can provide fertile ground for follow-up questions with even more interesting answers.

> **TIP**
>
> Ask a few simple closed-ended yes-or-no questions to warm up the conversation, then ask more open-ended questions about people's motivations that begin with "how come," "why," or "what." You'll be surprised at the interesting answers, and they may lead to some great opportunities for both of you.

Diplomacy Can Stave Off Disaster

Sometimes we don't enjoy an event but we have to be diplomatic because preserving a relationship can be more important than complete honesty.

Your friend has been raving about how she has found a wonderful recipe that you really must try, and she invites you over to dinner. You understand that Jessica has never been much of a cook. You know her best for her love of takeout and fast-food restaurants, and you've had many phone conversations while she's seated at the local burger joint, literally chewing the fat while chatting to you about her day. And now she wants to cook you a lavish dinner? You're not convinced, but to support Jessica, you accept the invitation and head to her place with expectations that at least the company will be good. When you get there, Jessica is still in the middle of cooking. "Hey, don't worry," she yells at you from the kitchen. "This is going to be wonderful. Just trust me." *We'll see*, you think. The first course is undercooked. As you bite through the cardboard-like pasta, you try to smile encouragingly and commend your friend for her efforts. "Hey, well done on the starter. So we're having three courses? Fantastic."

"How's the pasta?" she asks. You smile and nod, not wanting to have to tell a white lie, as you know she'd be hurt if you say you think it tastes like leather. You think the main course and dessert couldn't be much worse, but, unfortunately, they are. The vegetables are so overcooked they've almost disintegrated, and the dessert is crazy sweet. Didn't Jessica remember you're trying to wean yourself off sugar? Throughout the meal, she constantly asks for feedback. "How are you enjoying it? What do you think of the recipes?" You try not to seem ungrateful or critical by smiling, nodding, and keeping your comments vaguely positive. "Oh, I love carrots" (just not cooked until they're as soft as baby food). And "My mom makes a fab chocolate cake—I should get you the recipe!" (because it tastes 1,000 times better than this).

By the end of the evening you are tired as a result of staying so positive, but you know it's not worth hurting Jessica's feelings. You can see how much effort she has put into preparing this meal. You're happy you were able to stay vague and dance around her questions. Maybe next time you're out for a glass of wine and a few laughs, you can admit that it was an interesting experience, but for now you're going to use your skills of diplomacy to full effect. At the end you say with sincerity, "Thank you so much for the time and effort you put into that meal. It was so fantastic being with you tonight. I'm so grateful." Your friend is happy, and you're happy that she's happy. And all is well.

> **TIP**
>
> When you don't enjoy something but don't want to hurt anyone's feelings, you can be a little vague and make sure you find something to compliment, even when your overall experience wasn't particularly praiseworthy. Instead of referring directly to what you've experienced and voicing a negative opinion, simply refer to a general, more positive part of the experience and keep it light.

Don't Always Follow the Leader (Especially When They're a Gossip)

You're in a meeting at work with four colleagues and your boss, Tia. As the meeting nears the end, the conversation comes around to a friend and coworker who's not in the room. "What a joke," Tia says. "When I hired Jaime, I thought he'd be a fantastic manager and I imagined he'd be great within the accounts department. Well, I very quickly found out he's useless as a team lead. He has no charisma and no one wants to work with him. I had to give him his own department of one to limit the damage he'd do to the company. What a mess."

Everyone falls into an awkward silence. You've all heard about Jaime's struggles, and to some extent Tia might be correct. You don't want to be disloyal to Jaime by agreeing with your boss, but you need to stay on Tia's good side because she's known for being fiery and outspoken, and those who have crossed her in the past have been penalized or given a hard time. What's even more annoying is that Tia has lunch with Jaime several times a week, and they seem pretty close.

You decide that keeping quiet is the best policy. Your primary concern is that if any of you agree with Tia's comments, it may get back to Jaime, and he would be hurt.

As your boss finishes speaking, your eyes briefly lock and you nod silently to demonstrate you acknowledge and understand what she has said. You glance at your colleagues, and you can tell they don't want to be part of this conversation either. Your co-worker Allan is clearly embarrassed and isn't sure what to do. He laughs uncomfortably but stops when no one else follows suit. Although you don't actively choose to change the topic of conversation—after all, Tia is running the meeting—the lack of further comment defuses some of the tension. The awkward moment passes. Your boss changes the subject to a more positive one. Everyone looks relieved, and the meeting continues on to a close.

> **TIP**
>
> Try to avoid engaging in negative gossip. It might feel fun and harmless to join in, but think about how the person would feel if they knew what you were saying. It's better to keep quiet or walk away from that conversation.

CHAPTER THREE

Incisive Big Talk

In this chapter, we're going to dig a little deeper and explore some scenarios you might come across that involve more challenging conversations or subjects that might be difficult to broach. Whereas the previous chapter was concerned with small talk, the content in this chapter falls under the category of "big talk."

Give the Precious Gift of Encouragement

Do you have a friend or family member you love being around? When you're with them, do you feel on top of the world, even if you were in a bad mood beforehand? Perhaps you feel like that person is magical because they always manage to lift you up and bring out your best self. Why not try to be that uplifting person and boost the mood of those around you? It's easier than you might think!

You're chatting with your friend Jayden, and he reveals that he'd like to start online dating. He's never done it before and is a bit nervous. You know he's had a bad run of painful breakups and his confidence has taken a knock. Usually when he talks about his reluctance to get romantically involved and potentially hurt, you don't argue. But his eyes seem to twinkle when he talks about dating, and his voice has a hopeful note. He seems ready to dive in again, so you decide to give him some encouragement.

"Do you think I'm cut out for online dating?" he asks. "I like to stay home and read books—I'm a quieter type. Things move so fast these days. Maybe I'm too old-fashioned to find someone this way." It's a sensitive situation, and of course Jayden knows best when and how he should kick-start his romantic life. But you know he's looking for feedback, so you come up with some leading questions to help him see how wonderful he is and that he'd make a great partner. "What makes you think you're too old-fashioned to find someone this way? You're active in all those online forums on local politics, history, and conservation, and you seem to love connecting with new people. Why couldn't one of those new people be a romantic partner?"

Jayden says, "Maybe you're right. After my uncle passed a few years ago, my aunt ended up meeting her new boyfriend online. And one of my friends at work found her wife online, too. I'm not sure why I've been so hesitant."

"There's no reason it can't work for you!" you say, leaning toward him for emphasis. "Sure, you might have to go on quite a few dates before you meet 'the one,' but you're a great conversationalist. What negative things do you think will happen?"

Jayden considers. "Well, I don't want to get too sucked into it so I don't have any free time left," he says. "I can imagine it being quite time-consuming."

"Any other doubts?" you ask.

He continues, "Well, I won't want to jump in too fast with anyone. When you have an online profile maybe it's too easy to find things out about the person and make a snap decision, rather than learning more about someone over time."

After you ask a few more questions encouraging Jayden to think about things through a positive lens, he smiles and says, "Thanks so much for the pep talk. Your questions helped me dig a bit deeper and see that there's no reason I can't try it. If I don't take to it, I'll just take my profile down."

TIP

As humans, we tend to have a built-in negativity bias. Be the uplifter by challenging unfounded negativity when you hear it. A simple open-ended question can gently challenge a person's negative beliefs about themselves and can help them see things in a new, more positive light.

Create an Opening for Conversation to Bloom

Sometimes you can tell someone wants to talk but something is holding them back. Maybe they're not sure if they can trust you or they're worried that their opinion isn't fully formed. When you want to put a person at ease, you can take these steps to encourage them to continue.

It's late, and your 17-year-old daughter Sydney is about to head upstairs to bed. As she reaches over to kiss you good night, she hesitates. Sydney is usually pretty outspoken, and you can tell she wants to say something important. Even though you're both tired and she has an early morning ahead with her swim team, you want to hear what's on her mind.

"Hey, lovely," you say. "Do you want to talk to me about something?"

She hesitates. "No, I think it's okay. I'll go on up to bed."

You decide to press gently. Sometimes moments like these never return. "You know you can always talk to me. What's on your mind, honey?"

Sydney sighs. "Well, Mom, I know you really want me to stay on the swim team next year. You always come and support me and you've done so many early mornings getting me to the pool."

You think, *Oh no, she wants to stop. She's always loved it—in fact, she's on track to get a scholarship*. But you simply say, "I love you. It's a pleasure to support you and see you do so well," and then fall silent so she can continue.

"Well, I'm not 100 percent sure just yet—" She pauses again, and you remain silent until she continues. "I love swimming and I totally want to keep doing it, but I get so tired during the day at school. Sometimes I'm almost falling asleep during classes. I'm not sure how to cope. I know it's important for getting into college but I also don't want my grades to slip. I'm not sure what to do."

You want to jump in and suggest that surely there's a way to continue getting good grades while staying on the swim team, but you want to be sure your daughter has finished sharing. You've also always encouraged your kids to solve their own problems. You tell Sydney you appreciate that she initiated a potentially difficult conversation. "Honey, I want to thank you for bringing that up. I have my own opinions, but ultimately what I want is for you to be happy. Have you thought about how we can resolve this?"

"Thanks for hearing me out, Mom," Sydney answers. "I was so worried you'd be upset. I've been thinking about it, and I think I might be able to swap some classes to a different time-table so on swim days I don't have to do so much." She goes on to share her idea, which sounds reasonable. You resolve to talk about it more tomorrow, and she hugs you before heading off to bed. You are proud of her—and of yourself—for letting her express herself without butting in.

> **TIP**
>
> When you encounter someone who's uncertain about sharing something, create a clear opening. This can be as simple as saying, "Hey, you can trust me. I'd love to hear your idea/suggestion/story." If they start to speak and then stop, stay silent or gently prompt them to continue.

Summarize for Simplicity

Have you ever tried to make a point to someone but it doesn't seem to sink in? Do you find yourself discussing the same issues again and again, or circling back to the same old arguments? In these cases, a summary of your ideas or plan of action can really help.

For the past six months, you and your roommate have shared a small apartment. At the start, everything was great. You got along really well. You enjoyed the city nightlife together and even cooked meals for each other.

Your roommate is a night owl, studying for a PhD, and has plenty of freedom when it comes to her schedule. At first you were in a similar position, as you were unemployed and had a lot of free time. But after you landed a job, you had to get to work very early and realized you would have to restrict your nights out to weekends and holidays.

Meanwhile, your roommate continues to come home late, often with friends in tow, and to cook into the wee hours, involving much banging of pots and pans. She is generally insensitive to the fact that you're in bed at 10:30 p.m. on weeknights. After a couple of weeks of interrupted sleep, you decide to have a conversation. Your roommate seems to understand and nods thoughtfully as you explain that you need some quiet and that even with earplugs, sound still carries in the tiny apartment.

But the next week she brings home some friends at 2 a.m. They watch Netflix and comment loudly while you pull the covers over your head in the next room. You realize your talk was completely ineffective. The next weekend you share again that you really do need quiet and late-night Netflix parties have to be confined to the weekends.

You say, "I'm sorry to have to ask you to change your behavior, but can we please work something out?"

Again, she seems understanding. "No, I completely understand," she says. "You know I like my late evenings, but I love having you as my roommate, so I'm prepared to tone things down a bit."

"Thank you so much," you respond. "Let's summarize how we're going to move forward on this, please, just so we both understand. I realize it's a sacrifice on your part, and I promise to do whatever I can do to make it easier for you. I want this to be smooth for us both. I know I'm asking a lot, and I'm grateful."

She thinks for a minute. "Well, from Sunday to Thursday nights I'll keep the noise down after, say, 11 p.m., and I'll only invite friends back to the apartment on the weekend."

"Fantastic, I really appreciate that," you say. "And from my side, I can tell you in advance whenever I have a day off or a day when I don't need to be at work early so you can do your thing and don't feel you're wasting an opportunity to party."

"That would be great," she says. "We can even keep a schedule on the kitchen fridge. Are you okay doing that? Then there are no surprises."

"It's a deal," you say, relieved. You smile and hug your roomie. Hopefully the summary approach worked.

> **TIP**
>
> Summaries can be super helpful. They bring resolution to the discussion and make people feel heard and acknowledged. Ensure that everyone involved summarizes their point of view in their own words and that you all listen carefully and acknowledge what you hear to avoid further misunderstandings.

On the Same Team? Make Sure Your Stories Line Up

Have you ever been in a situation where you and a colleague or teammate were supposed to toe the party line but things fell apart? A simple check-in to share your opinions and accounts of the situation and a cohesive plan of action can avoid embarrassment, confusion, and wasted time.

Years ago, when I was living in New York City, I brought a taxi driver to court for stopping to pick me up and then driving on when he saw I was a Black woman. He pulled up just 10 yards away and invited another group to get in his taxi. They jumped in and presumably were soon home and warm, while my friend and I shivered in the winter night, cold and disgruntled.

I had clear sight of the driver's face and I thought my friend Andrea, who was with me, had seen it, too. She agreed to come to be a witness at the hearing.

At the hearing, everything seemed to be going according to plan. I shared my account of what had happened and clearly identified the driver. When Andrea stood up to speak, however, she admitted she hadn't really seen the driver's face. The case collapsed. We had both taken a half-day off work for nothing. The driver was free to go without punishment (although I hope he was somewhat chastened at having been summoned to City Hall).

I wasn't mad at Andrea for being honest about not seeing the driver's face clearly, but I was mad at myself for not checking with Andrea to ensure we had a leg to stand on. If I had realized she couldn't identify the driver, I may have thought twice about making the complaint.

In a courtroom, it's crucial for evidence to line up and not conflict. The same need for alignment applies, albeit more loosely, in a business setting. If you and a team member are going to present a united case in a work setting, it's critical to take a moment to ensure you're clear on your strategy and have lined up the details of your story.

Let's say you co-own a concierge company. Imagine a pitch for new business where the two of you are making a case to a prospective client. You want this client so much you're prepared to discount the service to make it seem more appealing. Your partner, however, feels that as a strong, potentially luxury brand, you need to keep your pricing high and should avoid giving discounts at all costs. With all the flurry of activity preparing your pitch deck and rehearsing the presentation, you forget to confirm that you're ready to present a united front during the question-and-answer session.

How will it look to your prospect if you share conflicting messages? Or if you disagree with your business partner during the meeting and end up having a touchy, under-the-breath discussion of your pricing and marketing strategies instead of being united in the presence of your prospect?

> **TIP**
>
> When working with others, make sure you align your messages before the big moment. If you're all on the same page, you're much more likely to achieve success, whether you're resolving a complaint, winning business, or convincing your kid it's time for bed.

Avoid "Shoulding" Others and Yourself

Do you enjoy being a voice of authority and telling people what to do? Although this may work in some settings, many independent types are strongly averse to, if not offended by, unsolicited advice.

My client Linda and her sister Flo sometimes have a challenging relationship. Linda is nearly a decade older than Flo, and though that difference counted for a lot when they were younger, today it doesn't mean much. Years ago, Linda was seen as the wise older sibling with great advice to be solemnly appreciated and absorbed. Linda realizes she still comes across as slightly patronizing, but these days Flo is quick to let her big sister know she can do things her own way.

I worked with Linda to help her avoid the "shoulds" when speaking with Flo. Linda sees she can get away with maybe one "should" per conversation, but any more and Flo's shoulders tense and her eyes roll. With a quiet tut, Flo will push back with a comment like, "Yes, I already know that" or "Yes, you don't need to tell me." Linda has been working at it, and now avoids shoulding all over Flo.

Can you relate to Linda? You have ideas for how someone might do something different, and the "You should try this" or "You should do that" want to fall off your tongue like commuters pouring out of a subway station.

Of course, using "should" or "ought to" might work with some audiences, but with others this approach will only succeed in putting their backs up, making them feel defensive and like a child in kindergarten being scolded by a teacher.

The "ask, don't tell" approach is a way to transform should into something much gentler. This strategy involves asking questions to get the other person to dig deep and find their own solution. If they ask for clarification or supporting detail, feel free to give a full response. But instead of saying something like "What you should do is . . . ," pose it as, "Hmmm, what's your knee-jerk response to this? What's the first thing you'd do?"

A wise coach knows their mentee has the answers within them and the ability to get to the correct answer. A good coach will steer or guide their mentee to the right answer and only tell them explicitly when necessary. This approach is especially useful for people who are proud or self-sufficient, as they are most likely to snap back if shoulded.

For example, contrast the following responses:

Should: *"Pam, why on earth did you park on the side of the street while you ran into the store? You should have parked in the parking lot! No wonder you got a parking ticket."*

Ask, don't tell: *"Pam, so sorry to hear about your parking ticket. It's tough when you only have a few moments to go to the store before picking up the kids. What else could you have done? Is there a parking lot nearby?"*

Being on the receiving end of a should is not enjoyable for an independent person who may have made an unwitting mistake and is capable of thinking things through (maybe with some gentle prompting). One final note: Even if you have a wisdom you'd like to share, consider the worst that can happen if you say nothing. Sometimes being an effective communicator means knowing when to simply smile, shrug, and stay silent.

> **TIP**
>
> Moralizing language like "should" and "ought to" can make others defensive. If you really want to help, take a coaching approach by asking the person what they might do if the situation played out again. They'll probably come up with an effective strategy and you can keep your shoulds to yourself.

Use Insight and Avoid the Inquisition

Have you ever had to conduct a job interview or get to know someone new, and all you wanted to do was ask question after question? The following account from my client Renata is a great example of how too many questions can be overwhelming and sometimes offensive.

Renata says, "I remember the first time I met my partner's family. I felt a bit like I'd been raked over the hot coals by his younger brother, Eli. In hindsight it's actually quite funny, but at the time I didn't appreciate all the questions and the focus on me at the dinner table in the picturesque seaside restaurant.

There were six of us at the table: me and my partner, his parents, and Eli and his wife. Eli decided he wanted to find out, in front of everybody, just how serious—or not—I was about his beloved older bro. He was truly checking me out, and he didn't care if I, or anyone else at the table, was aware of it.

Eli's questions came thick and fast. 'How old are you? How long have you been seeing each other? Where do you live? How did you meet?' I felt like saying 'Whoa! Calm down, now!' Instead, I diligently answered all the questions. Luckily my partner's mother took pity on me and occasionally added a few comments of her own.

After my response to 'How old are you?' she kindly interjected with 'Oh, you don't look your age, dear,' which made me smile and offer a silent thank-you. I've since gotten to know Eli quite well and he's actually a lovely guy. He's very friendly and sociable—not the hostile type at all. But that day I'd never have known it."

What could Eli have done differently? Perhaps he intended to make Renata feel like she was being assessed on her suitability for his brother, but I believe he was just curious. There's nothing wrong with curiosity, but nobody wants to be grilled. Rapid-fire questions can overwhelm the receiver. A more casual, natural approach is much more effective. Instead of conducting a question-and-answer session, it's preferable to offer a few insights of your own after your victim—oops, interviewee—responds in order to help them feel at ease. After each response, you can reply in a way that reflects or expands on the answer.

For example, if Renata had shared that she met her partner online, Eli could have said, "Interesting. Which site did you use? One of my good friends just started dating someone they met online, too," or "That's cool. Online dating makes it so much easier to meet someone these days. No more hanging out in bars trying to catch someone's eye like when my wife and I met."

Allowing a little bit of conversation between each question helps your subject recover, and they won't feel that you're in assessment mode. Information and insights flow freely in all directions and everyone feels they're learning a little bit about everyone else while participating in an enjoyable exchange.

TIP

Shooting off questions can make the other person feel like they're being judged or scrutinized. If you have things to find out, mix up your questions with tidbits or insights to put your interviewee at ease.

If Someone's Upset, Acknowledge Their Feelings

Do you know someone who tends to fly off the handle and get upset *quickly*? Although it can seem counterintuitive, instead of immediately trying to soothe them, try meeting them where they are before gently guiding them to calm down. This is called "pacing and leading." First you keep pace with them by acknowledging what they're feeling and fully empathizing. Then, you lead them toward a more positive emotion such as calm, acceptance, or hope.

Recently, my client Gabriela shared the following story: "The other day my partner came home agitated. He flung off his coat and announced that a potential new customer chose a competitor instead.

'I can't believe they'd do that to me!' he said. 'I've been working on this account for more than a year, and last time I saw them, they told me they'd definitely be choosing us. After all the time I put in giving them free advice, I can't believe they'd go with someone else.'"

What do you think Gabriela could have said next, using pacing and leading? And what would *you* do in the same situation? You could have said, in a cheerful voice and with a big smile, "Don't be upset, honey. There are other clients around the corner. Just wait and see."

But acknowledging and empathizing with someone's feelings tends to work better than trying to change these emotions. When people are upset, they need to feel heard before they can they move toward a more positive place. Instead, in a sympathetic tone, you could say, "Oh no, that's too bad. I know how much work you put into winning that account. I really feel for you."

To that he responds, "Yeah, think about all those late evenings I worked researching the company and all their products and making sure that our offer was a fit with where they're currently at. Jeez, I even missed Lukas's school recital because I didn't want to be a no-show at their product reception. What a complete waste of time."

As you watch your partner stomp around the room, you encourage him to keep talking about how he feels. "I'm really sorry. You so deserved to win that account. What happens next?"

"Yeah, I'm really disappointed," he says. "This account would have been a game-changer for the company and really fun to work on—we definitely could have helped them get back to being market leader." He starts to speak a little more slowly and quietly, and you can see he's beginning to calm down.

He sighs. "As for what happens next, well, I guess there are a few other accounts in the pipeline. I thought we had this in the bag. It's shaken me a bit, but I guess what we can do at the office is sit down and analyze why we didn't get it. I'm on decent terms with their head of purchasing, so maybe I can give him a call so we can learn what went wrong." Your partner's anger has started to blow over, and you can tell that he will soon be back to his usual cheerful self.

> **TIP**
>
> When someone is upset, don't try to *lead* them to a new emotion until you've first *kept pace with* them by acknowledging where they are and what they're feeling. They'll appreciate your empathy. Often, this will be enough to help them calm down a little. Then you can ask gentle questions or make suggestions to help them shift to more positive feelings.

Listen for the Message Underneath the Words

Wouldn't it be great if we could say what we mean and mean what we say? But in real life, people tend to use other words to mask the message and hope the listener is able to decipher the true meaning.

Perhaps the speaker is saying something uncomplimentary or controversial and doesn't want to spell things out. Maybe they are worried about how you will respond to a direct question—you could say no or disagree with their opinion. There may be other reasons people try to engage you in a roundabout way, such as to keep you talking and fill some time or to gauge your temperament in the face of challenging questions or information.

In this situation, you can choose to out the true meaning by saying something like, "Ah, do you mean . . . ?" or you can ignore the hidden meaning and take the comments at face value.

The situation could be as innocent as kids wanting to delay going to bed, so they keep asking you to read stories as a stalling tactic. Or it could be more serious, such as a colleague or relative who wants to make life difficult for you.

For example, your brother's wife, Pam, always takes issue with the fact that you don't live closer to your aging parents. You're grateful to your brother and Pam for helping look after your folks, but you have a family of your own and a job you love, and you're not prepared to move back to Chicago. Your parents have given you their blessing and want you to be happy. You send money, call them regularly, and visit when you can. But Pam can never let the subject rest. When you're together at Thanksgiving, she keeps making comments.

"Did your mother tell you she had a fall last week? Well, I'd imagine you're so busy with that fancy job of yours as sales director that you wouldn't have had the time to worry about it anyway." Pam looks at you pointedly. "But luckily I wasn't far away and was free to help her."

You had heard about the fall and called your mother immediately, and you also followed up with her doctor. You debate whether to tackle Pam's comment head-on or let it go. Her accusations are hurtful but familiar. A couple of years ago you might have taken her on, but these days you try not to take the bait.

"Thanks, Pam," you say. "I'm glad you were there—your help was very much appreciated. Please know that despite the challenges of my job, I'm *never* too busy for family." Your conciliatory tone deflates Pam's argument. She shifts uncomfortably, not wanting to accept your gratitude, then changes the subject to her daughter's high grades at school.

How you respond to these hidden or partial messages is really up to you. If someone is making a veiled accusation or trying to bait you, you have to decide if you want to take the high road and ignore the negativity, or shine a light on what's being said and deal with it directly. If the conversation is happening in front of others, you may want to speak privately to your antagonist. If you're dealing with a bully, however, sometimes it helps to stand up to the person publicly to show you're not intimidated. Weigh the pros and cons and make the call that works for your situation.

> **TIP**
>
> People sometimes disguise their message or just want to needle you and provoke a reaction. Listen for the underlying meaning and motivations behind what's being said before you decide how to respond. You may want to get to the bottom of things, or you might just take the speaker's words at face value and move on.

Let Someone Know They Hurt Your Feelings

Recently, your consulting company took on a new client with a very aggressive project deadline. Although your team worked hard to meet the first milestone, they handed in the deliverable a little late.

During the next client meeting, when their representative asked why the work came in late, your manager said that it was partly your fault and did not acknowledge any responsibility as team leader. You were shocked because you generally have an excellent working relationship with your manager, but you chose not to argue during the meeting. You try to let it go, but after consideration, you decide to let her know her behavior was unfair and hurt your feelings. But how do you go about doing so?

It's important to choose your words and timing carefully. Blurting out accusatory, poorly considered comments can make things worse. The next time you see your manager in the hall, you feel your blood boil. You want to scream something like, "How could you do that to me? Your behavior was completely out of line. We know it wasn't my fault and I can't believe you'd be so outrageous as to point the finger at me. You are ridiculous and I never want to work for you again!"

Take a deep breath. This is not the place. You don't want to dig yourself into a hole or get in a shouting match in front of all your colleagues. Instead, think about how to open the conversation and express your hurt and indignation in a less emotional way. It's good to take a deep breath, look your manager in the eye without smiling so she knows you're serious, and start with something positive such as, "We've had a fantastic relationship for the past two years I've been on your team, and I really enjoy working with you." Starting with positivity provides a cushion for a challenging situation and communicates that you like and respect your manager generally, but you are troubled about a particular situation.

Remember to own your feelings. You can do this by starting your sentence with "I feel." Instead of saying, "In that meeting with the client, you really threw me under the bus and it was outrageously unfair," you could say, "I feel that it was unfair to point the finger at me and let the client think it was my fault we didn't hand in the document on time. It was a team effort. I think everyone was responsible."

It's important to be aware of your intentions. Before you address the situation, take a moment to consider why you're sharing that your feelings were hurt. Do you want to get it off your chest, or make your manager feel guilty? Or do you want to prevent the situation from recurring and get back to a good footing? Realize you may not achieve your desired outcome. For example, you can't force your manager to apologize. However, the gentle "I feel" approach should prevent them from getting defensive so they can clearly consider your point of view.

This approach allows you to express your feelings without being accusatory. You're not in control of your manager's response, but you can act with dignity, restraint, and assertiveness.

> **TIP**
>
> If you need to tell someone they hurt your feelings, start on a positive note and let them know you appreciate them before sharing what was painful about the specific situation. Always own your feelings with an "I feel" statement rather than pointing to how the other person behaved.

The Essential Skill of Saying I'm Sorry

I've always liked the Elton John song "Sorry Seems to Be the Hardest Word" because of both the music and the sentiment. Even when we know we messed up, it can still be difficult to apologize. There are also times when we feel we did absolutely nothing wrong, but know that a simple "sorry" will help patch up the situation.

Make sure your apology is sincere. We frequently observe celebrities or public figures who have offended others on social media offer an apology that doesn't actually express remorse. In a graceless and stilted way, they'll issue a statement such as, "I'm sorry [that random famous person or social group] took offense at what I said."

This isn't a true apology because it's doesn't actually own the offensive behavior. A better statement would be something like, "I apologize for what I said about vegan burgers. I realize my comments upset a lot of people, and I see now how offensive I sounded."

In a way, it's easier to apologize in writing because you don't have to see how the other person responds. But it's far better, if possible, to apologize face-to-face. This approach takes guts, but the other person will see you care enough about the relationship to look them in the eye.

A sincere apology makes it clear that you understand why what you said caused unhappiness or upset. This helps the other person feel understood and defuses the conflict. The right apology might look like this: "I apologize for revealing that you're getting married before you had time to tell the rest of our group. It was really unacceptable behavior for a best friend and I totally see why you're mad at me. That news was yours to tell."

The wrong apology would look like this: "I apologize, *but* I knew you were going to tell everyone the next day so I didn't think I was doing anything wrong," or "I'm sorry, *but* you know I can't keep a secret, so you should have known better than to tell me." The word "but" negates the apology and takes you back to where you started. The gracious apology accepts responsibility and doesn't try to justify your behavior.

Once you've apologized, you can ask for forgiveness and then wait quietly for the person to respond. It can look like this: "I'd love to get back to where we were. We've been friends for so many years. Please, can you forgive me? I'll make sure never to violate your confidence again."

Be prepared to accept that they may take a while to warm up to you again. They might even vent or get angry and emotional about how you made them feel. This is a normal reaction, so be sure not to interrupt to defend yourself. You might even need to have this conversation several times more until you're fully forgiven.

In extreme cases, you may never be forgiven. But at least you know you offered a generous and wholehearted apology. Let them know you'll be there waiting and are holding space for them to forgive you, however long it takes.

> **TIP**
>
> When you need to apologize, there's a time to speak and a time to keep quiet and listen. Don't try to justify your behavior, as doing so will only dilute your apology. Instead, be generous and wholehearted, even if you feel you didn't do anything wrong. Saving the relationship is usually more important than proving a point.

Ask for a Pay Raise or Promotion

It can feel greedy to ask for a pay raise or a promotion, but it's a necessary part of being employed. If you don't receive regular salary increases and recognition, your entire career may be affected. But how do you broach the subject *and* achieve the desired result?

Some of the following strategies can also apply to freelancers and business owners who are providing price quotes for their services.

You need to build the value of your work before asking about the goodies. It's important that your boss or potential client understands your strong points and the benefits you bring before you start talking about compensation. In his book *Jab, Jab, Jab, Right Hook*, serial entrepreneur and media mogul Gary Vaynerchuk notes that you must give before you receive. Once you have some time and achievements under your belt, it's time to book the meeting.

To start the conversation, ask your boss some open-ended questions that highlight the value you've brought to the organization. "Thanks so much for agreeing to this meeting today. I love working here, and it has been a fantastic opportunity to be involved with some of the most high-profile projects over the past year or so. I'd love to hear how you think I've impacted those projects."

When your boss shares that she has seen and heard good things about your contributions and she is pleased with the way things have gone for the company and your role in making this happen, you can build on her response by sharing some specific details about your accomplishments as they pertain to your firm's progress.

"The Riverside project was especially exciting, and the idea I contributed regarding marketing regionally as well as locally helped the team reach our sales goals more than three weeks ahead of schedule and exceed our targets monthly from then on." Your boss nods in agreement. "Also," you continue, "we picked up a new project with Riverside's sister development because of the success of the first project, which means more work for our company, an expansion in the number of employees, and an increase in the bottom line."

"Yes, that's very true," she concurs. "And that project is twice the size of Riverside. I was very happy when we won that business."

Now is the time to strike. "I'm so glad you were happy about that," you continue. "That said, I've been in the role of junior marketing exec for the past nine months, and I feel like I've proven my value to the company time and time again. Commensurate with that, I'd like to propose a 10 percent pay increase, which, though insignificant relative to the increased revenue that's coming in after our success with Riverside, will help reflect the increased responsibilities I've been taking on.

"I'm also eager to be promoted to senior marketing executive. I've got some great marketing ideas we can apply to some of the new projects that will really make a difference. Being senior exec will also help my ideas carry more weight in meetings and the team will be more likely to adopt them, which will benefit us as a company as well as our clients."

Your boss nods thoughtfully and you breathe a sigh of relief that you asked. Now wait to hear what she has to say.

> **TIP**
>
> If ever you ask for more money, a promotion, or new business, always start by building your value in the other person's eyes first. Ask open-ended questions that steer the conversation in the direction of your skills, the problems you've helped solve, and the benefits of recognizing you.

Disagree with Dignity—Without Damaging Your Relationship

Did you ever disagree with someone, and later feel your relationship never got back on the same footing? It's important to prevent a simple disagreement from creating a seismic change in the relationship.

When you have conflict, it's important to separate the opinion from the person and consider how important it is to be right. One strategy that can prevent serious conflict is to use sentence openers like "From what I've seen" or "I tend to think," rather than hard lines like "Everyone knows that" or "It's obvious that." These gentle openers make it clear that you understand not everyone feels the same way you do, and it's fine for the other person to disagree.

For example, you always dread going to your mother's house because your stepfather is opinionated about your decision to homeschool your son and always tries to pick a fight with you.

"So what are you teaching your boy at the moment?" he asks. "I know for a fact he's missing out by not being with other kids his age. He spends way too much time with his mom."

"What do you mean?" you ask, attempting to counter his objection. "I think that during a child's formative years it's important to be in a nurturing environment, and the local schools can't always provide that support."

"That's baloney," he responds. "Kids these days are too soft as it is. What he needs is for you to enroll him in the local school as soon as possible. Don't play around with his development."

You're fuming. How dare he tell you how to raise your child? If this man was anyone else, you'd grab your things and leave, but for your mother's sake you know you have to maintain a relationship with him. You decide to take the high road and avoid arguing. It's time to close the conversation down. You decide to acknowledge the comments and show some respect, but you don't have the energy or the inclination to go back and forth for the next hour on this topic with someone who isn't going to change. Ultimately, it's your decision.

"Brandon, you know I respect your views, and I appreciate that you have my son's interest at heart. I think we could debate this topic all day long. I get that you had a very positive experience when you were at school and you hold strong opinions about how kids should be educated. However, my opinion is different. In the same way I respect you, I hope you can respect my views, too. My boy is happy. He's learning and doing really well. That's what I care about. Maybe there's no right or wrong in this conversation. Kids can flourish no matter where they learn, so let's agree to disagree, shall we?"

You end with the best smile you can muster to let Brandon know there are no hard feelings, and you hope he won't push back and try to keep needling you. "Right," you announce. "I'm going to go grab some drinks. What would you all like?"

> **TIP**
>
> If you want to disagree respectfully, it can help to acknowledge that you fully understand the other person's viewpoint. This will disarm them and stop them from repeating the same arguments. State that you don't have the appetite for disagreement, then firmly change the subject.

○ ○ ○

CHAPTER FOUR

Discerning Body Language and Facial Expression

Although it's impossible to quantify their impact, tone of voice and body language reveal a great deal about a speaker and their intentions. This chapter shows you how to improve communication by watching the gestures and expressions of others and using body language.

The Art of Acknowledging Negative Nonverbal Communication

Sometimes it pays to watch nonverbal responses even more closely than we listen to the words being said. When we are alert to the flicker of a raised eyebrow or a slight change in voice pitch or rate of speech, we receive extra input that can help us decide what to do or say next.

Some people struggle greatly with reading even the most obvious body language and verbal cues. Have you ever seen a person just not take the hint, even when faced with a frown, pursed lips, folded arms, and other negative body language that screams "no"? Conversely, the change in facial expressions may be subtle and quickly disguised, but these, too, can be telling. In 1967, clinical psychologist Dr. Paul Ekman coined the term "micro expressions," or facial expressions people reveal in a microsecond before we have time to compose ourselves. The primary expressions are fear, disgust, anger, happiness, contempt, and sadness. When the words you hear don't seem to tie in with their facial expression or body language, let nonverbal communication guide you.

Have you ever been the underdog? Maybe you're going for a promotion at work, but you know all the other candidates are older and more experienced. You carefully watch the interviewer while you verbally recap your résumé. When you discuss your short time at the company and mention that you graduated only a year ago, you see the interviewer frown and his shoulders stiffen. His body language had been friendly and open, so this tiny change is a clue that your interviewer might be responding to evidence of your lack of experience and possible inability to do the job.

In a situation like this, it can pay to acknowledge negative nonverbal cues. After all, they are clues. Use the situation as an opportunity to share your strengths. You might say something like, "You're probably thinking, why did I interview for this job? Well, I know I'm the youngest in the department and have been in this position for only six months, but let me explain some of the ideas I've introduced and the positive impact they have had on our results."

You go on to describe them, then summarize with, "I believe I bring fresh ideas and a new approach that make me more than qualified for this role."

You might notice your interviewer's body language change from tense to more relaxed. You voiced what he was thinking and feeling, brought his concerns out into the open, and defused them with evidence supporting your pitch. This strategy is always good. When problems or challenges are hiding under the surface and unspoken, they're much harder to resolve. If you can spot and address them, pat yourself on the back—these are good communication skills at work. Your interviewer will likely be impressed that you were astute enough to identify and discuss these silent concerns, which demonstrates empathy and emotional intelligence. After you've moved beyond your interviewer's concerns, you can then go on to share (with humility, of course) how great you are and why he should choose you.

TIP

When you're in a conversation, watch for nonverbal signals. Whether negative or positive, acknowledge and respond if you can, almost as though they were spoken words. Counter a concerned look or a frown with some positivity.

When Silence Beats Small Talk

Although small talk can be great for getting to know someone or breaking the ice, sometimes you're just not interested in shooting the breeze with the person next to you on the bus. Maybe you're studying for an exam or preparing for an interview. Perhaps you have a splitting headache and the last thing you want is to indulge in chitchat. You don't want to hurt people's feelings and seem rude, but you also have to consider your own peace of mind and well-being. Using nonverbal cues can be an excellent way to convey your disinterest in small talk.

For example, you're sitting in the office breakroom having lunch as you mentally rehearse for the pitch you're giving to a potential new client later that afternoon. By your plate is an index card with some key bullet points. This will be the first time you've taken the lead role when pitching for new business. You're going through your opening lines and figuring out what kinds of questions you might be asked in a couple of hours.

At least you were, until Li from the purchasing department decides to sit across from you. With a broad smile he asks how you're doing. You smile warmly without saying anything, as you don't want to break the flow of your thoughts, and hope your expression conveys kindness. You quickly glance at your notecard and hope that he understands you're in the zone.

He looks at you quizzically, still smiling. "You're quiet today. Is everything okay?"

"Yes, thanks," you reply. "Got a big pitch coming up later today and I'm doing some last-minute homework." Again you look at your notecard, hoping he'll get the message. Unfortunately, it still doesn't work.

"Oh, a pitch?" he continues. "That's interesting. Who's it for, and who's on your team? Did you hear that we recently won that telecom company as a client? I thought Joy and her team did a fantastic job. I'm sure you'll be just as good this afternoon. What's the main thrust of your pitch?"

Uh-oh, you think, wishing you'd taken your lunch to your desk. Your subtle clues aren't working. You're going to have to do more to let Li know it's really not a good time for a chat. You smile again, adopt an apologetic expression, and grimace slightly while tapping your crib card. "I would love to chat some more, Li, but I only have an hour before we present and I need to work out a few things in my head."

Li finally gets it. "Oh, I'm sorry, I didn't take the hint." He looks embarrassed, and grabs his tray. For a moment you feel sorry you'd mentioned it, but you're also glad you were honest. He glances around the room. There are no free seats. He says, "There aren't any other free tables, so would you mind if I sit here and eat my sandwich without talking to you anymore? And hey, good luck later!"

You smile. "Thanks, Li." You're glad you were able to let him know in a gentle and respectful way that this wasn't a good time to talk.

TIP

If you don't want to talk, sharing fewer words than usual can convey that it's not the right moment. A warm or rueful smile and gentle nod or gesture can often be enough. If you couple these gestures with some well-chosen words, you won't hurt anyone's feelings.

Quiet Someone Before They Put Their Foot in It

Do you know someone who is a bit short on tact or tends to say the wrong thing, especially in front of a group? If you need somebody to just *stop* speaking before they say something offensive, *the look* can work wonders. The look is a combination of a frown, brief shake of the head, and tightening of the lips that means "Not now!"

My friend Sunil is one of those people who is curious about everything and can't hold back his questions. His partner, Lorenzo, likens him to a five-year-old boy who wants to know about the world and doesn't understand that some things are best left unsaid, or at least held back for a private conversation. In fact, Lorenzo has developed his own version of the look to use when Sunil is in danger of saying something that will cause offense or create a situation.

When Sunil is about to make a blooper, the look is usually enough. But for extreme cases, Lorenzo also developed the follow-up look, which employs a shocked glance with raised eyebrows and flared nostrils. Sometimes he even puts an index finger gently to his lips. It initially looks like a shushing gesture, but Lorenzo quickly curves the finger downward and leans forward so he looks like an intellectual deep in thought. When Sunil sees the follow-up look, he backs off and gets the scoop on the journey home.

The look tends to work most effectively with a close friend or family member who won't take offense at being silenced. If you can agree that they're a fairly frequent offender and they are open to it, you can follow Sunil and Lorenzo's example and work out a secret code that means (in the kindest way) "Shut up! I'll tell you why later." When you're formulating your sign language, remind them not to ask you what's wrong or what you are trying to hide, as this can be even worse than the comment you are trying to prevent. Persuade them to trust your judgment that following your lead is the best course of action to avoid a faux pas. Cite the maxim, "Hold your tongue now, laugh about it later. Speak now, regret possibly forever." Another sign that can work in these situations is gently squeezing their hand or arm.

> **TIP**
>
> A subtle look can often be enough to steer someone away from asking a disastrous question or saying something negative to the group. If someone close to you tends to put their foot in their mouth, consider creating your own secret message that says, "Hey, you're digging yourself into a hole. Stop talking. I'll tell you why later."

Pick Up the Pace by Pacing

Energy and enthusiasm are persuasive traits. When words alone aren't doing the job, an easy way to grab people's attention is to stand up and start moving around the room with purpose. This can work in both the personal and work setting, whether you're trying to convince others to join you on an outing or accept your idea for a project.

Let's say you're at work with a room full of colleagues and you've been explaining why it's so important that the new traffic-calming project you've been researching gets funded. You're sitting around the table in the boardroom with everyone else. But you decide it's time to raise the energy level and help everyone see just how important it is that this initiative gets the green light.

All the contributors before you have presented good projects worthy of funding. You wonder how you can emphasize how important yours is. You decide to employ a secret weapon that no one used. Everyone else has delivered from a seated position, but you don't have to follow suit.

As you get to the most important part of your project—that putting it in play will save lives—you want your body to match the passion of your words. You push back your chair and stand up.

"This project is so important and needs to be implemented as soon as possible." With the word "so" you extend your arms wide to show the magnitude of its significance. You then slowly walk around the table, detailing some of the stories of those who were injured or worse at the dangerous junction. Then you stop. All eyes are upon you, engaged with your words and sensing your passion.

"This project could be implemented in just three months. The investment required is small, but the effect on the lives of area residents would be huge. The right decision today will save lives!" You reach out your hands, palms up, in a gesture that says, "Please believe me!" You glance around the room, making firm eye contact with each person, one by one. This solemn eye contact ensures that everyone gets the message. Your face is relaxed but unsmiling.

You know words alone sometimes aren't enough—their delivery can be vitally important, too. When you stood up, your movement and gestures made your argument much more powerful. Everyone realized you were prepared to go out of your way for your ideas to be noticed and adopted. By gesturing with outstretched arms and looking your colleagues in the eye, you conveyed trustworthiness, authenticity, and passion.

You slowly walk back and take your seat. Later, when it's time to vote on funding for each project presented, yours gets approved. After the meeting, several colleagues commend you for your boldness and they tell you how effective you were in backing up the intensity of your words and purpose. Your motion drew them in and made them listen more closely.

TIP

Nonverbal body language, such as standing up or moving around while you speak, can add intensity, energy, and surprise to your message. It shows commitment to your words, and is an effective way to get people to pay attention to you.

Let Your Body Say No Before You Speak

Did you ever talk to a stranger who seemed a little too keen to become good friends? Or a new business colleague who acted like they'd known you for years and was being just a tad too familiar? Or perhaps you went on a first date where your suitor was clearly more enamored than you? Sometimes other people move a little too fast. In these circumstances, body language can be a valuable tool to convey the message that you want them to slow down.

Picture this: Your sister has set you up with one of her colleagues. She's been singing his praises for months. Apparently, he's fairly new to town, has a great smile, and is an excellent cook—or seemed so from the sensational homemade lasagna your sister said he brought to the office holiday potluck.

So here you are, enjoying dim sum at a local restaurant. Jorge certainly has a great smile and seems super friendly, but he's trying way too hard. It's awkward. You mentally kick yourself and make a note to find your own date next time. It's so much harder to extricate yourself without causing offense and disappointing your date and your sister.

Jorge is leaning across the table, smiling broadly and sharing that he's so happy to have finally met you and can't wait to get to know you better. "Hey, have you tried that new sushi place near my office?" he asks. "Maybe that's a good location for next time?"

Not so fast, you think, wondering how you can dampen his enthusiasm a little. You haven't necessarily decided against a second date, but you want to think about it before making a decision.

You smile at Jorge briefly, but with a little reserve showing. The smile doesn't fully meet your eyes, and you hope your expression reveals you're not 100 percent certain that there will be another encounter. Instead of holding his gaze for a long moment, you look at your plate, fold your arms in front of your body, shift in your seat, and pause before responding. You hope this combination of signs is subtle enough that you're not necessarily heading to the sushi place—at least not with Jorge. You look up again, make eye contact, and say, vaguely, "Yes, I've tried that restaurant. The food is lovely." But you don't answer his question about next time.

Jorge blushes slightly. His gaze skitters away from yours. "Uh, oh, well," he stammers. "Your sister has told me so much about you that I feel I know you well already. Sometimes I can get ahead of myself. I'm sorry." A long, awkward silence follows.

Whoever said dating is easy needs to be here with me today, you think. You resolve to be noncommittal but warm for the time being. After all, Jorge was paying you a compliment with his interest. You smile, uncross your arms, and say, "Hey, it's okay. Remind me to kill my sister next time I see her! Ah, look, here comes dessert. Yours looks delicious!"

TIP

There are sensitive situations in which we need to gently say no. You can use body language like breaking eye contact or folding your arms to distance yourself without using words. Most observant people will pick up on these gestures and spare you an awkward dialogue.

Warmth that Goes Beyond Words

As a consultant and communication coach, I often work with clients to help them become more comfortable with public speaking. The work we do preparing them to speak can be very helpful, but sometimes a client is attacked by nerves midway through their big speech. It's easy to spot. Words that were flowing suddenly dry up, or they begin to look a little uneasy as self-doubt creeps in. When I'm present, it's my job to switch to silent encouragement mode. You can do this, too.

My client Genevieve is a delightful woman from France. She speaks flawless English with a warm French accent. But like many who speak English as a second language, she sometimes feels like she's not communicating properly. She worries that her word choice could be more sophisticated, or that her accent will get in the way of her message's effectiveness.

Genevieve was making a presentation at a workshop I was running. She got off to a strong, confident start and the audience was fascinated by her motivational message. However, partway through her presentation, Genevieve suffered from a sudden bout of self-doubt. Her voice wavered and she seemed to lose track of what she was saying. I knew it was time to give Genevieve a nonverbal boost so she could get back on track.

When Genevieve's eyes settled on my face, I made strong eye contact and smiled broadly as if to say, "Wow, I'm loving every word of what you have to say." I nodded, too, in a wordless but emphatic agreement with the opinions she was expressing. Noticing my encouragement, she quickly found her place again and carried on with vigor and clear direction. Next time she looked at me, I smiled again and made a thumbs-up sign to say, "Fantastic, this is perfect!"

Sometimes people need wordless encouragement to continue. Whether someone is making a presentation to a group, speaking up in a small meeting, or even talking in a one-on-one conversation, we can help them feel encouraged and spur them on. Maybe a junior colleague wishes to speak during a meeting but isn't as confident as your longer-standing colleagues. You can employ the same tactics to encourage quieter people to continue speaking once they've started. Smile, nod, and silently urge them to continue when they pause or stumble, or when their words seem to dry up. If your colleagues attempt to interrupt, a simple gesture like a raised index finger to silence their interjection can encourage the speaker to keep going and show them they have supporters in the room.

> **TIP**
>
> Sometimes words are not enough. People respond to positive cues, so show them you want more of the same by nodding enthusiastically, smiling, and showing positive energy with your stance, gestures, and openness.

Not Too Heavy with the Handshake

The handshake is a sign of connection and openness, an opportunity to show you are a friend who can be trusted in life and business. According to *National Geographic*, handshakes originated at a time when people frequently carried weapons for their protection. The shaking of hands, palm to palm—knife, gun, or bow and arrow aside—conveyed a message of peace and trust and indicated a desire to strike up a genuine relationship.

Since that time, the handshake has become a universal gesture of connection, whether between friends or strangers, and almost always regardless of rank. Even royals such as the Queen of England have been known to shake hands with their guests.

If you are offered a handshake, it's important to get it right. Too limp and you may seem uninterested or wimpy. Too strong and you might be trying to show them who's boss. The way we swoop in for the handshake can also be telling. If you maneuver so your hand is on top, you might be seen as dominating or manipulative. It's amazing how so much can ride on a simple gesture. But in Western society, many a first impression has been made and many a business relationship and a friendship have been floated or sunk based on the quality of that initial handshake.

Be careful not to let overenthusiasm turn into a bone-crushing display of strength. If you feel your knuckles crack, something went wrong. When a person comes away from shaking your hand looking like they're in pain, or yelping like a dog whose tail has just been trodden on, it's time to lighten up. But if you go too far in the opposite direction, you can come across like you have no enthusiasm for the person you've just greeted.

Practice your handshake with a friend or colleague. Tell them you want to get it just right and ask them to share their honest assessment. You may feel a bit silly practicing such a universal gesture, but better to get it right than to learn you were sending out the wrong impression.

Be aware that in some situations and cultures, a handshake may not be automatic. Sometimes a warm smile or a nod of the head and a few words of greeting may be enough, or a clasping of the arm or gentle pat on the shoulder.

> **TIP**
>
> Limp handshakes are off-putting and a sign of disinterest or weakness. A firm (but not bone-crushing) handshake is the goal. Realize that for personal or health-related reasons, people might alternatively nod, or use a fist bump, elbow bump, or toe touch.

Let Your Feet Do the Talking

Did you ever struggle to get away from a chatty person? You do your best to politely indicate that you need to leave. But they keep talking. And talking. You find yourself mentally screaming for them to stop so you can get away, but you're too nice to break in until it's too late, so you have to interrupt in a very obvious, unsubtle way. And you're the one who ends up feeling impolite. In these cases, a simple tool like the direction of your feet can help get your point across.

It's the monthly happy hour for your office and you're out with your colleagues, talking about the weekend ahead. You don't have a lot of time to hang out, as you have to pick up your daughter from track practice, but you decide to stay long enough for a quick bite and a few minutes of conversation. Your colleague Aaron is in the middle of one of his stories. Everyone loves Aaron's tales. And he loves telling them. So much so that he takes it very seriously when someone doesn't hang on his every word. That's why you take pains to explain that you can't stay much longer even though he's deep into his story about being lost in Peru.

"Hey, Aaron," you try to cut in. "This is a great story! I can't wait to hear the end, but you do know I have to run, right?" Aaron pauses. He is leaning in, intent on sharing how he feared for his life. His hands are gesturing widely and he has a huge smile on his face that says, "I'm in my element here."

You decide to use your body language to let Aaron know you genuinely do have to leave. You take a step backward, physically distancing yourself from Aaron and his story. But he only steps in closer. *Okay, that's not going to be enough*, you think. You take another tiny step back and fold your arms, creating both distance and a barrier between you. Aaron keeps rolling and shows no signs of slowing down his tale.

Then you decide on a different tactic. You point your feet away from Aaron so your legs look like they're about to walk you away. Aaron starts to take the hint. He continues to speak, only faster. You dig around your bag, trying to find your car keys. You did warn him, and you don't feel guilty for not paying rapt attention.

You purse your lips slightly and stop nodding, holding your head stiffly to one side, as if to say, "Sweetie, are you done?" Eventually, even Aaron knows to quit. "I guess you really do have to go?" he asks. "You can't even hang on for the bit where I stumble upon a local village and they invite me to stay for the night under the stars?"

You uncross your arms, hitch your bag over your shoulder, and jangle your keys. Your body is now fully turned away from Aaron. You look back briefly, shake your head, and deliver some parting words. "Sorry! I definitely need to hear the end of this one, but it's going to have to wait. Not sure if you've seen my daughter in a bad mood, but it's not pretty when I'm late. We'll have to get lunch together next week and you can put me out of my suspense." With that, you give him a wave and a warm smile, and you're gone.

TIP

If you're not engaged in the conversation or you need to leave, point your feet away from the speaker. This subtle move indicates you're ready to walk, so when you do, it's not so jarring. This action signals the speaker to start winding up. Once they take the hint, you can soften the impact with an apology or explanation.

Grab Your Server's Attention

Sometimes you're at a bar or a restaurant and you can't get the server's attention. Body language can definitely help in this situation. Making gestures to catch the server's attention, tracking their movements with your eyes until they feel the intensity of your stare, or even shifting in your seat can work wonders.

Recently my client Wei was on a business trip. He had been traveling all day, and he couldn't wait to get checked in and settled for the night. He was really looking forward to a relaxing meal at the hotel restaurant, where he could warm up and chill out. Unfortunately, the restaurant had only a couple of waitstaff, one of whom was doubling as the bartender, and a table of 12 people was being seated. Wei figured this large group would take up most of the staff's energy and attention, and he might have to wait longer than anticipated.

He strategically chose a table in the middle of the restaurant and watched the waitstaff hustle past him several times without acknowledging him. So he decided to move to an even more prominent spot. Looking around, he could see several patrons also sitting alone looking frustrated, as if to say, "Hey, isn't my money good enough to get your attention?" One woman even stalked out of the restaurant, clearly convinced the long wait wasn't worth her time.

Wei could see that sitting back and waiting wasn't going to work, but he was determined not to leave the hotel and brave the cold. It was time to do a little more to get some attention. His new table was within eyesight of the bar, so he stared at the bartender. The young man briefly caught Wei's eye, but made no move toward him.

It was time to use the sit-forward-and-wave technique. Wei sat up with his back erect, looking like a schoolteacher watching his pupils with an eagle eye. A waitress tried to pass by without acknowledging Wei, but he raised his hand and waved the menu in the air.

The waitress smiled as though she had all the time in the world. "I'll be with you in just a moment, sir." But "just a moment" turned into another 10 minutes. Wei gritted his teeth. This experience was getting more stressful by the moment. Eventually he walked up to the bar.

At the bar, Wei waited with a serious face. When the bartender approached him, Wei pointed to his table and asked, "I see you're busy, but can you please serve me?" He was direct and serious, but not rude, as there was no need to be rude or cause a scene.

"That's where you're sitting, sir? Please go and relax at your table and I'll be over as soon as I can."

By the time Wei got back to his seat, one of the other travelers had also given up and left. Wei was glad he hadn't waited passively or lost his cool. He eventually got served. It wasn't as fast as he would have liked, but he did realize his goal of enjoying a good meal in a warm environment.

> **TIP**
>
> In a bar or restaurant, if you're not being served as quickly as you like, nonverbal communication is a great way to get noticed. Gestures, facial expressions, and a general air of impatience or frustration can help garner attention. But never forget to express your thanks and understanding.

A Simple Touch Says So Much

Sometimes it's difficult to know the right thing to say, whether it's to convey solidarity, sympathy, or support. And sometimes there's nothing we can say, but we can use touch to convey what's in our hearts. This form of personal contact bypasses awkward statements and is striking in its simplicity.

Over the past few weeks, you can tell your colleague James has been under some pressure. Eventually one of your managers announces that one of James' children is gravely ill.

You want to support James, but as someone who doesn't have children and who hasn't yet had a relative or friend with a grave sickness, you're not sure what the etiquette is for expressing sympathy. You want to acknowledge his situation with a personal comment.

The next time you see James, you walk over to his desk and say hello. You give him a gentle pat on the shoulder while making eye contact with a sympathetic gaze, and you say, "I'm really sorry to hear what your family's going through." Although you didn't say much, you hope the brief physical gesture transmitted your feelings. James looks at you and nods. "Thanks. I appreciate that. It's been a tough time, but everyone here at work has been great. So supportive."

You're glad you didn't try to express yourself with a lot of unnecessary words. You like to communicate in an authentic way, and the physical touch approach felt like the right choice.

The key with physical touch is to keep the gesture brief— and appropriate. A lingering finger drawn down the inside of someone's arm can convey something very different than a quick pat on the shoulder. If you're in any doubt as to whether your intended gesture is appropriate—especially if it's in a work setting or if you don't know the other person well—you can offer a handshake instead and use your facial expression to convey your emotions.

Touch doesn't have to be limited to conveying sympathy or empathy. A fist bump is a good show of solidarity in a casual situation. Sometimes clutching someone's hands and smiling into their eyes can be a great way to celebrate their good news, such as an engagement, the birth of a child, or a new job. Other expressive gestures include a gentle pat on the back, a brief squeeze of the forearm or shoulder, or even a slight tap on the back of the hand. The key is to couple the gesture with the right facial expression so both are congruent.

TIP

When you need to show solidarity with someone but don't know what to say, a simple light touch, accompanied by a sympathetic facial expression, shows you care without words.

Let Your Gestures Win the Battle

Have you ever felt like you've repeated your words so often, but no one is listening and you need another approach? Gestures, body stances, and facial expressions can be particularly useful in these circumstances.

Your 15-year-old daughter, Yuki, is going through a rebellious phase. No matter what hour you set as her curfew, she extends it without permission, coming home later each time. You have tried explaining why you've set these curfews and are worried about her getting home safely. You've even offered to pick her up, but she turns down your offers.

You've had long and reasoned conversations, but Yuki doesn't want to listen. You hope this phase ends quickly. Last night she came home at midnight instead of her 10 p.m. curfew. You were worried sick because she didn't answer your calls, and things escalated when she walked in the door.

"I told you to call us if you're going to be late. Have some respect! Your dad and I both have to work, and we're worried sick when you don't come home on time or answer our calls. We don't want any harm to come to you. Please listen to us. I hate arguing with you like this. You're old enough to be responsible and to realize it's not all about you!"

Your daughter screams that she's old enough to look after herself. The argument continues to burn until your daughter screams, "I hate you!" Deflated, you sink into a chair, trying not to remember the troubles you gave your own parents when you were the same age.

The next day, your daughter is late again. But you resolve to use a different strategy to convey your disapproval. Yelling and screaming doesn't help anyone, and it's making the home atmosphere very stressful. You decide to use silence instead of shouting to make your point.

As Yuki enters through the front door, you stand in silence. You let your face convey sadness and shake your head slowly. You meet her defiant glance with a flat expression before looking away. Your body and face say, "I'm disappointed and tired. This is not the relationship I want to have with you, but you leave me no choice."

Your daughter has never seen you this way before. She is used to fiery arguments, but your deflated stance takes the wind out of her sails. You can see her wondering how to respond to this new behavior. You can see she's startled by your reaction and can tell she doesn't want to hurt you. "Mom, I'm sorry," she says. "Can we talk about this in the morning? I don't want to make you upset anymore."

Wow, you think. *Maybe the silent approach works better with Yuki.* You look forward to the fruits of your conversation in the morning and resolve, going forward, to let your body and face speak rather than your words.

TIP

When you're caught up in a war of words, but you feel everything to be said has already been shared, you can use your facial expression, body language, and a skeptical look to indicate that you're fed up with fighting.

Use Your Body to Deliver Bad News

Body language and facial expressions can help cushion bad news. You can let someone down gently rather than issue a big, resounding "no." Nonverbal communication can signal your decision before you confirm that your response is not the desired one.

Your son has decided he'd like to host a huge party to celebrate his 18th birthday. You're happy to help him arrange a celebration, and you suggest taking some buddies out to a local restaurant or having a sleepover for three or four of his good friends. Instead, he has his heart set on turning your house into a nightclub and hosting a rave for 40 or 50 guests. Given that you've just installed new carpets and furniture in your den, you are firmly against these plans, but he's a good kid and you don't want to disappoint him.

"Mom, it would be great!" he says. "We could clear out all the furniture and put it in the yard. I know a guy who's an amazing DJ and could bring his sound system over. His speakers are huge—we wouldn't need music anywhere else in the house. I'll make sure I clean everything up the next day. Anyway, even though I'd invite maybe 60 kids, probably not all of them would show, and you know my friends are respectful, right? They'd never trash the house. You can trust me on this!"

How can you say no? First, you fold your arms to signal you're not wildly excited at the prospect of 50 kids in your house. You tighten your lips slightly to give your face a slightly disapproving air. You say nothing, but you hope that your son can see you're not on board.

"Mom, I can tell you're not convinced, but hear me out." Your son then goes on to note that his friends are an incredibly responsible group of teens and he would personally warn each and every one to take special care of your new white carpet.

At this point, you allow your face to relax into a slight smile. You curve your lips, but the expression in your eyes is serious and says, "I'm sorry, honey, but no can do." At the same time, you shake your head slowly but firmly. You stand with your legs firmly planted shoulder-width apart as if to say, "I'm not moving on this one. I stand firm and sure." Your raised eyebrows say, "You can keep talking but my mind is made up." You breathe out in an audible puff of air. Your posture, gesture, and expression communicate that you heard every word and you want to please your son, but it's not going to be possible on this occasion. Your son realizes resistance is futile.

"Oh Mom, please?" he begs. "Okay, okay, I understand it's a no. All right, let's talk about other options. It would have been the best party! Maybe next year, before I go to college?" You breathe a sigh of relief that your son took the hint. *Maybe next year will be fine, but we'll cross that bridge when we come to it*, you tell yourself.

TIP

Dissenting body language can act as a powerful cushion to soften the blow of a soon-to-be-spoken no. Make sure you telegraph your thoughts and opinions with very clear and easy-to-interpret nonverbal expressions, such as raised eyebrows, pursed lips, shaking of the head, folded arms, and a strong, firm stance. Combined, these signs deliver a powerful message without the need to say a word.

CHAPTER FIVE

Salient Written and Visual Skills

Sometimes we don't have the luxury of being in the same room as the person with whom we are communicating. This chapter explores a variety of written and visual skills you can use to get your message across when you can't rely on visual props and physical gestures.

Email Signatures: A Great Place to Shine

Do you have a side business? Do you love motivational quotes? Perhaps you recently won an award or you strongly support a charity. Kind of like your own personal bumper sticker, your email signature is a great place to share a bit more about yourself and what you stand for. Your place of business may dictate what goes in that space. But for personal email accounts, or if you don't work for a company, personalize and publicize as much as you want.

A business coach I worked with was fanatical about listing her current press and social media mentions in that spot. I've seen others use the space to feature their favorite quote to brighten someone's day.

If you don't use your email signature for something dear to your heart or that you want the world to know about, you could be missing an opportunity. You don't have to change it frequently. Just make sure it's something meaningful to you.

Do you doubt that people will scan this area below the main body of your email? Think again. I have tracking software that tells me if a link in my email signature has been clicked, and most people are curious enough to check it out.

An email signature is also a good conversation starter. Maybe you have a fascinating fact about yourself or a personal project you want people to know about. Maybe you just had a baby and you'd love people to see his cute little face. You can post links to a few of your social media profiles and ask people to follow you. Pretty much anything goes. You can publicize events, new products, a fundraiser for your kid's school, or the results of your favorite sports team.

This isn't about bragging, but sharing. If you want to share something fun but you don't want to reveal much about yourself, you could post a quote from a character on your favorite TV show or a link to a song you love.

Make sure the signature is easily visible, clickable (if necessary), quick, and easy to read. The signature shouldn't be longer than the message itself. I try not to distract with flickering GIFs, but if that's your personal style, go for it. And if a link takes readers to another site, instead of pasting in the raw URL, rename it so it's clear what people are clicking on. For example, instead of your link saying www.bighitx3455s, which tells us nothing, rename it something like, "Check out the song that's number one on my playlist" or "My brother wrote a song—take a listen."

Also, the email signature isn't the place for a dense paragraph of text (unless you work for a legal or financial company). Better to go with a few well-chosen words or links and make it easy for the reader to scan and click on what interests them.

If you haven't yet used this key bit of real estate, what are you waiting for? Jump into your email settings now and per-sonalize, personalize, personalize!

> **TIP**
>
> Your email signature, or even your social media bios, can be a fun and effective place to share your personality and preferences. Add some information about what's important to you, whether it's a quote, a link, a book you've read recently, or the good cause you hold dear to your heart.

Use Clothes as Communication

What's your style? Take a moment to think about your wardrobe. Are you the casual type? Maybe you love to dress up and be flamboyant with bright or patterned fabrics and unusual cuts or combinations.

Whatever your preference, think about selecting your clothes in a more purposeful way so they project how you want to be seen. We've all heard the expression "dress for success." Of course, success means different things to different people and in different industries. A computer programmer is unlikely to turn up for work dressed in formal attire, and someone in commercial banking may be expected to wear a suit to the office.

If you're angling for a promotion at work or you want to level up your social life, make sure your clothes coordinate with your intended destination. Don't dress for the job you have. Dress for the job you want. Observe the people you work with whose style you admire. I recently heard about a young guy who worked in a bank. Desperate for a promotion, he got a haircut, started to dress more formally, and tried to look the part. When the next round of promotions was announced, he was given the role of junior manager. Presumably his work was good enough, too, but his sharp appearance helped him stand out from others at his level.

Casual doesn't always mean junior. Years ago, the more senior you were, the smarter you would dress. These days, that idea has been flipped on its head. Chief execs often wear very casual clothes. The items may have designer labels, but they are far from the three-piece-suit-and-tie mold. Early in his days at Apple, Steve Jobs wore more formal attire, but during later keynotes, he became known for his casual attire of black turtleneck, jeans, and running shoes. The higher you rise, the more leeway you might have with your outfits.

In the meantime, the right clothing can give you confidence. One of my former clients, Kay, loved to wear colorful and eye-catching combinations. She always stood out from the crowd, whether she was making a presentation or seated in the audience. Her appearance conveyed that she was confident, creative, and different. But when I got to know Kay, she described herself as shy and needing a way to find her voice.

"I know the way I dress shouts out that I'm bold and brave, but I really don't feel that way," she explained. I suggested that she let her style do the talking and allow the outward confidence she showed to permeate inward to help her relax and feel that same sense of creativity, fun, and joy.

Clothes are a form of communication. Humans are visual creatures and prone to many biases. What kind of message would you like to convey when you're speaking at a conference on behalf of your company? How do you want to be seen during the business pitch you're booked for next week? When you go to have dinner with your partner's parents, will you choose to wear anything different than usual? Think about how you want to be seen and whether your clothes are fit for the purpose.

> **TIP**
>
> Humans are visual creatures, and the items you wear on your body are a wordless message. Your clothes can say so much about you, whether they make a statement about who you are as a person or how you're feeling on a particular day.

Let the Image Do the Talking

Do you ever use slides or presentation software? Most people use the text on the slides as a prompt. You create slides packed with words and think, *I don't need to learn this presentation. I'll just read each word verbatim and that'll save me the time of having to rehearse.*

The problem is, your audience can read those slides, too. And if they can read what you're saying, you might as well not be there. Your audience is faced with four choices:

1. Try to both read and listen

2. Listen to you speak and ignore the visuals

3. Read the slides themselves and forget trying to listen

4. None of the above

The fourth option is when you lose your audience and they surreptitiously look at their cell phones or imagine what they're going to have for dinner.

Instead of loading your slides with text, let the image do the talking. Recently I was training employees at a successful event management company to pitch successfully and win more opportunities to organize conferences, events, and parties. Each staff member had to create and present a dummy pitch.

Many presented densely packed slides containing more text than the Bible. These people were suddenly transformed from lively, outgoing professionals to robotic, static readers. This was easily remedied, however, because one thing events companies often have in their arsenal is fantastic imagery. Photos from huge parties with fire eaters and acrobats. Images from weddings held at gorgeous sun-drenched foreign locations with attendees savoring the event of a lifetime. Professional photography from lavish corporate events with great lighting and sets so elaborate they could only be staged in aircraft hangars.

The same principle applies outside the event industry, too. If you're telling a personal story of a trip you took, bring the talk to life by showing a photo. Do you have a story about a relative? Include their picture. Maybe you work in the data industry? Share graphs that tell a story and are easy to interpret, and supplement the data with your message.

There are some great sites online with free photography you can use, several of which are listed in the Resources section (page 132). You can even use comic images, provided you have a license to display them.

The right photo can convey a mood, a vibe, a feeling, or an emotion. Give the image its own full slide and allow your spoken words to complement what's on screen. Yes, it will require a little extra work to create the commentary and to memorize your key points, but the effect will be so much more impactful.

> **TIP**
>
> If you have to create a slide deck or presentation, think about how you can let your images take center stage. It may not possible on every single page or slide, but wherever you can, make it easy for your audience to stay engaged.

Keep It Light for Texting

We're so lucky to have a variety of ways to communicate with those around us. We can meet in person, on video, via a voice call, and, of course, through text and instant messages. But not every form of communication is created equal, and each has its uses. If you have something important to say or if there is a risk of misinterpretation, I highly recommend using voice or video to communicate.

With text, even the most harmless message can turn into a monstrosity. A client of mine, Belinda, was chatting with an old friend, Riley, who's a mother of two children. Riley's a great mom, and Belinda would never criticize her parenting skills, but somehow a harmless exchange of text messages about what they were having for dinner went sour.

Belinda messaged Riley and asked what she was planning to eat. Riley was going to cook for her family, whereas Belinda was waiting for takeout. As long as Belinda had known her buddy, Riley had always loved eating out. So Belinda texted, "Hey, it's good to cook sometimes," meaning what a nice way to spend your Friday, cooking for your family.

But Riley thought Belinda was implying that she rarely cooked a decent meal for her kids. She heard, "It's good to cook **sometimes**," not "It's **good** to cook sometimes." Riley got defensive and accused Belinda of being patronizing.

After a long flurry of texts, Riley realized Belinda was trying to be supportive and affirm her choice, not accuse her of being a lazy mom, which hadn't even crossed Belinda's mind. Both women ended up peeved. Belinda was irritated that Riley would think she'd be unkind, and Riley felt defensive at even the hint that Belinda was criticizing her mothering skills.

The friends eventually ironed things out, but Belinda resolved to keep all future text messages simple and clear. Belinda promised Riley that going forward, she'd keep her most significant exchanges to voice or in person. Riley didn't disagree.

You might pride yourself on being a clear communicator and feel that your texts are never misinterpreted, but someone might take offense at a seemingly innocent comment. If you get a sense that this is what's going on, jump on the phone or meet up as soon as possible to clear things up.

> **TIP**
>
> Avoid serious discussions via any medium where brevity is key, like text messaging. Often, the quest to be brief or succinct can lead to unclear communication, which can lead to misunderstanding and conflict. If things look like they're getting heated, quickly take them offline to a voice conversation or in-person meeting.

A Scrap of Paper Can Hold a Mountain of Meaning

Not everyone enjoys big surprises. Some people hate to be the center of attention. A surprise party or a jumbotron proposal can provoke pain rather than pleasure. But for just about everyone, small, touching tokens of affection can be a lovely way to let someone know you care and are thinking of them.

For example, after a few years of raising your children, you have your first job interview in what feels like ages. You've told your family how nervous you are about reentering the workplace. When you get to the security desk, you reach for your photo ID and feel an unfamiliar piece of paper. You take it out and unfold it. Written across it is a message from your son: "Mom, you're the best! Good luck. I love you."

The thoughtfulness of the message moves you almost to tears, and you smile at the thought of how lucky you are and the support you have waiting for you at home. You approach the interview with a spring in your step and feel proud of your kids and excited about showing off your skills and competencies. Regardless of whether you get the role, you know you have a team that loves and supports you.

It takes just seconds to write a quick message, but it can have a profound impact on the recipient. Do you have someone in your life who needs a boost? Consider sending a little message of support or love. It could be a single-sentence email to a team member at work who's going through a tough time, taking on a new challenge, or preparing for a big presentation. "The board won't know what hit them—you're an ace!" Maybe you pop a note in your child's lunchbox wishing them good luck on their spelling test and reminding them of the spelling of a tricky word. "You're an awesome speller! You'll MESMERIZE your teacher!"

It could even be a note slipped under the door of the roommate you exchanged words with the day before to let them know there are no hard feelings and you're eager to get back on a friendly footing. "I know we disagree sometimes, but you're a great roommate. Want to meet for dinner tonight? My treat. :)"

All these messages are random and unanticipated, and that's where much of their impact comes from. You can create messages like these on a regular basis and vary who you send them to, or change up the message or where you hide it. Figure out who needs a boost this week, and make a point of lifting them up. As a bonus, you'll likely find that sending these messages is uplifting for you, too. The message doesn't have to be in your own words. If you don't consider yourself to be much of a wordsmith, motivational or thoughtful quotes can deliver the message you want. Does your partner have a favorite author? Go online, grab a selection of their quotes, and pop them into your secret messages. Do you enjoy poetry? Look up some of the best lines from your favorite poets and use these. The possibilities are endless.

> **TIP**
>
> Small, unexpected notes telling a friend or family member you love and support them or sharing some encouragement are a great way to deepen your relationship and create some surprise and delight.

Time to Take Your Complaint Public?

These days, we can find reviews for anything, and companies are especially sensitive about their reputations. This can certainly be a benefit to us as consumers because we can learn about a company, product, or service before we invest. And when we're not happy with how we're treated and our complaints are ignored, we can go public with the tap of a button. Social media can amplify our message and help us air our grievances to tens, hundreds, or even thousands of people, increasing the likelihood of our issue being resolved rapidly and in our favor.

A doctor friend was flying to Germany and needed to catch a connecting flight. His first flight was delayed, so he missed his connection. Although he had alerted the airline of the tight time frame before the initial flight left the airport, nothing had been done about it. He ultimately had to purchase a different flight from another provider in order to get to Frankfurt with enough time to enjoy his weekend.

My friend was frustrated about being ignored and paying out of pocket through no fault of his own. After various conversations with both airlines and calls to customer service, he was still disappointed by the lack of a sympathetic or helpful response.

Many companies have teams of people in customer relations whose job it is to monitor the company's reputation on social media, so my friend turned to Twitter. You might not expect a simple tweet, with a half-life of 24 minutes, to be an effective vehicle for a complaint. You might feel like you're dropping a teaspoon of salt into the ocean and expecting it to be noticed. But the airline quickly sent him a direct message offering compensation in exchange for removing his post. *Voilà!*

Information travels fast, and a single negative comment can be devastating to a company. Once you've tried all the usual methods to get your complaint heard, posting your issue on social media can be an excellent alternative, or follow-up, to a dissatisfying customer service experience.

News outlets and consumer groups agree that making complaints on social media can be very effective, and even offer guidelines on what to say:

1. Use the company's name and social media handle within the post for maximum exposure.

2. Keep the comments brief and to the point.

3. Be courteous in choosing your words.

4. If you don't receive a timely response, make a follow-up post and mention the lack of response.

5. Ask family, friends, and colleagues to share your original post.

For complaints, use a channel where you can post short, sharp messages. You won't have to hang on the phone or write long, explanatory notes. Customer services departments prioritize publicly available communications ahead of emails, phone calls, and letters. Keep in mind that not all companies are on social media, and check that the company whose attention you're trying to grab is on the platform you intend to use before posting your message.

> **TIP**
>
> If you're not receiving the customer service attention you require, Twitter might be a good place to turn. You may receive a speedy response from a customer relations representative whose only job is to preserve the reputation of the company.

Please Do Not Disturb!

Can you concentrate on the task at hand even when the roof is falling down around you? Or do you need time to resettle at the slightest interruption? According to a 2015 study by Gloria Mark, it takes nearly 30 minutes for the brain to settle back into its original task after some kind of distraction. This lag time can be hugely problematic for productivity and even for emotional well-being. Now imagine being interrupted four or five times during the day, and think about the impact this will have on your ability to get things done.

How can you avoid these kinds of disruptions, even though you may welcome distraction as it can be a lot more enjoyable than slogging through our workload? Use a visual signal to let people know you can't be disturbed. Consider the following example:

You're working from home during a massive blizzard. Your kids and your partner are in the apartment, too. You'd usually jump at the chance to spend some quality time with your family, but you have to turn in a report by 4 p.m. at the latest.

As much as you've tried to explain to your six-year-old that Daddy mustn't be disturbed, your message just hasn't sunk in. Your little one has come up with an absorbing new game of knocking on your home office door to get some attention, and running away giggling when you appear with a frown that quickly becomes a smile because you can't stay mad for long.

Try using a sign. Create a printout with a photo of Daddy at work with colleagues and pin it to the door. When your kids see it, it means you're doing office work and no disruptions are allowed. You can also try installing the red light, as mentioned in chapter 1 (page 16). As an added incentive, hand out a small reward when your children stick to the rules.

You can do something similar at work. That colleague of yours who simply can't resist stopping by for a quick chat whenever he passes your desk? Explain that when he sees the photo of you collecting last year's award for best sales rep faceup on your desk, it means you're working on trying to win the same award and he should not disrupt your focus.

When my partner is working from home, he settles down to work right away and is incredibly focused, whereas the sound of a passing vehicle is enough to break my concentration. He doesn't think twice about interrupting me because it's not an issue for him, but these little chats throw off my productivity like crazy. I usually close the door of the room I'm in to indicate that I'm working and he shouldn't interrupt. Quite often he ignores me, but at least I try!

TIP

When you need others to give you some space, a simple sign or note can do the trick. Whether that's a red light, a closed door, or a sign at your cubicle, make sure you share upfront in a nonemotional way what the sign means, then use it to create some space.

Just Like Diamonds, Social Media Posts Are Forever

Social media is powerful because so many people can see your messaging, but it's important to remember that social media can also create a very public and lasting perception of you. Don't rely on deletions. There are apps that store and archive deleted posts, so once your post is up it may be too late to make it disappear entirely. The best way to manage public perception is to carefully curate your social media profiles.

A friend of mine, also a speaker, had a bad experience with a global brand and decided to vent about it. Instead of unloading to a friend or a family member, however, he chose his very public Instagram profile to grumble about the quality of the company's products and state that he generally didn't like the brand and preferred a competitor.

Years later, when my friend applied for a speaking opportunity at an event that the brand was running, he wasn't selected, even though he was well-qualified. When he asked why, he learned that his throwaway comment, which he had forgotten, was the reason.

Although it's up to you what you complain about and where, this scenario illustrates how practically everyone can see social media posts. If someone wants to find out more about you and is prepared to dig deep and take time, they can learn a lot. Like a diamond, many posts last forever. However, if you're grumbling or making negative or potentially damaging comments, then your post is less like a diamond and more like a tarring—long-lasting, but not in a good way.

We've all heard stories of public figures who shared controversial opinions before they were famous. When a big opportunity later came up, like running for public office, presenting at the Oscars, or representing a global brand, someone unearthed the unsavory comments and rallied for the celeb to be dropped from that high-profile role or campaign.

You may not have any aspirations to be a celebrity, but reputation matters. Nobody wants to risk losing a job or facing backlash for something they communicated without thinking or during a heated moment. Before posting online, always run a quick mental check. Ask yourself:

Am I in the grip of a strong emotion? If you were calmer and more relaxed, would you make the same post? If the answer is no, wait a while before posting to make sure you still want to.

Will anyone be offended by what I'm intending to post? If being offensive isn't your intention, rewrite the post or simply don't post it. Sometimes writing your thoughts can be satisfaction enough without sharing them.

Will this bite me later? If you were to be promoted, or one day find yourself in a more public or influential role, would you still make that post? Are you 100 percent ready to stand behind what you've said and completely happy to own that comment?

Our moods change, our circumstances change, and our views change, but the comments we make publicly live on and on. Though it can be tempting to vent, choose these moments with care—and preferably with a few trusted individuals rather than on a medium the whole world can see.

> **TIP**
>
> Social media can usually be seen by anyone and everyone, friend or foe. If you're sharing something you don't want freely available forevermore, reconsider your message or your audience.

Weigh the Risks with a Public Proposal or Gesture

Do you have a big message you want the world to see? In this very public age, individuals who want to stand out from the crowd and cut through the noise have to make gestures that are grander and more audacious than ever before. But this behavior carries comes risks.

For example, you may choose to announce to the world, with weekly or daily countdowns to "D-Day," that you're quitting your job and taking up the laptop lifestyle—only to find yourself back home after a couple of weeks, embarrassed and deflated, because the money ran out or you didn't like it (the latter happened to a friend of mine who had planned to move to Australia and live by the beach as a surfer dude).

Or you might decide to make a very public declaration of love to that special someone, only to become horribly embarrassed and angry, or, worse still, deliver a very public rejection. You may have seen a marriage proposal at a big sporting event using a jumbotron to convey the message. Somebody might find this approach tacky, but it's unarguably a big gesture and the drama can be exciting. You have to make the call—unforgettable or lacking in intimacy? It can certainly make for some fantastic photos for you to show friends and family. So, with this bold and brave gesture, what could go wrong? It's worth thinking this through beforehand.

In the laptop lifestyle example, it might be humiliating to be back home months or years earlier than you'd planned, but at least the only person affected is you. However, if you're proposing marriage or making a gesture that involves others, it's also important to consider the other person's feelings and what can occur if things don't go according to plan.

For example, with a jumbotron proposal you're possibly putting your partner under immense and unwelcome pressure. If they're not 100 percent sure about marriage (or you), surely they'd rather have the opportunity to talk it through in private than to feel thousands of eyeballs staring at them. How hard would it be to say no under those circumstances? Maybe in that moment they utter an emotional "Yes!," but that response might take you only as far as the parking lot.

If your significant other is more of the feisty, spontaneous type, you might even get a "no" right there in the stadium. You'll want to be ready for that, and then expect for your proposal (and potential rejection) to go viral because some people are entertained by the misfortunes of others. Be sure your loved one is the type to appreciate such a public display of affection and that you've thought through that you might become a social media phenomenon for a while after your proposal—regardless of whether it's accepted.

> **TIP**
>
> If you're placing a message in a very public place, think through the implications of sharing it with so many people, from both your perspective and that of your intended recipient. Be ready for what could happen if you receive a very public rejection, or if you have to change your plans (everyone will know you didn't follow through).

A Simple Formula to Keep Work Emails on Track

I love sharing little frameworks and models with my clients to help them get to the point quickly and easily, and to make their messages clear and digestible. Nowhere is this skill more important than at work. Have you ever received a long and rambling email from a colleague that either hadn't been thought through properly, or was so packed with unnecessary details that you just stopped reading? Instead of helping solve a problem or contributing positively to an issue, these emails tend to cloud matters. Why is the message being sent? What's the underlying message? Who is supposed to take action when it has been sent to multiple recipients? What should be done in response to this email, and when? Questions, questions, questions.

The What, Why, and Now framework helps keep email directives clear and specific. **What** stands for "What's going on?" **Why** represents the question "Why should you care and pay attention?" and **Now** signifies "Now what should you do?"

This framework is so handy and effective for keeping emails on track that I know of large multinational organizations that require all their employees to use this format for outgoing messages.

So how can you use this yourself? Let's make it about something fun, such as a colleague's going-away party. She's moving to a different city and you're in charge of getting a group of coworkers together to give her a celebration she won't forget.

You quickly type out an email: "Hey, everyone, are you free on March 18 for Carmen's send-off celebration? We've been thinking about where to go and haven't decided yet, but we all want to find a great location. Any ideas? Make sure you all clear your calendars for this one, as Carmen has been at the company for 10 years and she's been responsible for lobbying for flexible working, as well as being the best supervisor on the planet and always being there to support us through challenges. I'm not sure what we're going to do without her! And let's gather some funds to buy her a lovely gift she can keep forever that will remind her of working with us. It's going to be a great celebration, so please tell anyone else you think might like to come along, but don't tell Carmen. It's a surprise!"

Instead of sending an indigestible block of text like this one, use this simple framework to make your email punchier and easier to absorb. (I've prefaced each part of the example on the next page with "What," "Why," and "Now" for clarity, but there's no need for you to do the same!)

> **TIP**
>
> When communicating by email, make it quick and easy for people to know why your message is relevant and what they should do in response. Frameworks and guides like What, Why, and Now make this task easy and take the guesswork out of writing, and are formatted in a way that's simple and effective.

What (what's the point?)

Carmen's Going-Away Party

March 18 after work. Save the date!

Why (why should you be interested?)

Carmen is leaving the company for new adventures. She's been a wonderful team lead, lobbying management for many of the benefits we now enjoy, such as flexible working, and is much loved. Let's give her a send-off she'll never forget.

Now (what should you do next?)

How you can help:

1. We still need a venue, preferably a restaurant with a private room that can seat around 30 people for dinner. Have ideas? If so, please email me back ASAP with your suggestions.

2. We're collecting funds for a gift for Carmen. If you'd like to make a contribution, please speak to Stephen.

Finally, save the date, and don't tell Carmen! This is a surprise party. RSVP by March 10.

CHAPTER SIX

Moving Forward

Congratulations and thank you for coming this far. You're loaded up with examples and scenarios to spark your ideas for how to communicate in all kinds of situations.

You've learned when and how to employ simple but effective communication skills that will help you feel confident and in control across the myriad areas of daily life. The strategies you explored in this book are easy to grasp and don't require sophisticated communications. The key to improving as a communicator is to use these tools as often as you can, and check back here for reminders. The more you adapt these strategies to various situations, the more they will become second nature. Eventually, you won't have to think about them anymore; instead, they'll be close at hand whenever you need them. You may even find yourself sharing your tools with others. The world runs more smoothly when we communicate better.

Taking Stock

Let's recap some of what we explored:

We looked at **verbal communication strategies**, like tone of voice, whether friendly, assertive, or otherwise. We also explored the power of compliments and how to make an introduction to a stranger. Other skills include rephrasing thoughts before we speak, and providing feedback constructively as a way to help solve problems, display empathy, or defuse conflict. We talked about what we can learn from listening to another person's tone, how we can stay positive in conversations, and when the best course of action is silence. We discussed how asking open-ended questions can provide encouragement and convey a willingness to listen.

Some of the **nonverbal communication strategies** outlined in these chapters include having a friendly smile with strong eye contact, maintaining erect posture, and keeping body language open or closed, depending on the message you wish to convey. We talked about the power of standing up and moving around when we speak, and how gestures can be a stand-alone form of communication or add punch to words. We explored simple frameworks to help organize emails quickly and easily, and increased awareness of the right platform for the right message; for example, how avoiding text messages when discussing weighty or emotional topics can prevent misunderstandings.

As discussed early on in this book, the key communication areas of our lives fall into three main categories:

1. Casual interactions with acquaintances and strangers.

2. Day-to-day contact with work colleagues and those we spend time with through nonwork activities such as volunteering, sports, church, and social pursuits.

3. Our interactions with friends, family, and loved ones.

When we think about the fact that all these three categories of interaction can take place in person, on the phone, online, or via some kind of written communication, it's clear that we have a lot of different permutations to deal with. There are enough options here to keep you practicing and sharpening your skills for the rest of your life.

Now that you've completed this book, take out your list of the different people you come into contact with on an average day ("Who Do You Talk To?" on page 8). For the conversations and connections that you'd like to improve upon, list a few communication strategies you can try during these interactions. For example, if your work colleague always tends to interrupt you, list a few ways you can be more assertive. Write down when you'll next see this coworker, and decide how you'll change your behavior to let them know when you shouldn't be interrupted.

Your Intentions as a Communicator

Underpinning all the skills and scenarios we've talked about are your intentions as a communicator. These intentions will vary from situation to situation, but ultimately you'll want to ask yourself:

- What outcome would I like from this interaction?

- Do I want this person to see me as a supportive and friendly champion of their idea, or is this unimportant?

- Do I need to get my point across quickly and succinctly without concern over the response of the person I'm communicating with, or does their opinion matter?

- Is it my intention to appear strong and in control, or relatable and friendly?

- Do I need this person to know I don't agree but want to convey it in a gentle way, or is it okay to generate some friction here?

Don't be afraid to pause before deciding on a communication strategy for a specific situation. Take a breath before you send off that feisty email so you can discern whether what you've written will irritate your colleague or get them to comply with your idea. Listen and gather your thoughts while you decide how to cope with your boss's temper tantrum. Reread that social media post and make sure it says exactly what you mean without causing offense.

As we go through life, sharing, negotiating, agreeing, disagreeing, and connecting, our ability to communicate clearly and expressively is incredibly important to who we are and what we want. At a time when the prevalence of short-form messaging is making it more difficult for people to connect on a human level with understanding and confidence, your skills at big talk, small talk, and everything in between will make life and relationships easier and help you stand out as a thoughtful, effective communicator. I wish you the very best as you move forward, communicating with grace and confidence!

Resources

To see videos related to this book's content, visit SholaKaye.com/bigtalk.

Books

Captivate: The Science of Succeeding with People **by Vanessa Van Edwards** (New York: Portfolio Penguin, 2017)

This book will help you take charge of your interactions. You'll learn about storytelling, reading people, and so much more.

How to Be a D.I.V.A. at Public Speaking: The Step-by-Step System to Engage Your Audience and Present with Confidence **by Shola Kaye** (Jacksonville: Movement Publishing, 2017)

Need to do any public speaking? This straightforward guide will help you with everything from planning your talk to delivering with confidence, and it comes with a free video course.

How to Talk to Anyone: 92 Little Tricks for Big Success in Relationships **by Leil Lowndex** (New York: McGraw Hill, 2003)

This witty book is an essential guide for hitting it off with people quickly and easily.

Speak to Influence **by Susan Berkley** (Campbell Hall Press, 2004)

Want to work on your voice? This book is full of exercises for intonation, diction, and more.

Free stock photography

Gratisography.com

Pixabay.com

Unsplash.com

Studies

For more on micro expressions, see PaulEkman.com

References

Croston, Glenn. "The Thing We Fear More Than Death: Why Predators Are Responsible for Our Fear of Public Speaking." *Psychology Today*. November 29, 2012. PsychologyToday .com/us/blog/the-real-story-risk/201211/the-thing -we-fear-more-death.

Eckman, Paul. "Universal Facial Expressions of Emotion." *California Mental Health Research Digest* 8, no. 4 (Autumn 1970). 1ammce38pkj4ln8xkpliocwe-wpengine .netdna-ssl.com/wp-content/uploads/2013/07 /Universal-Facial-Expressions-of-Emotions1.pdf.

Eisenberger, Naomi, Matthew Liebermann, and Kipling D. Williams. "Does Rejection Hurt? An fMRI Study of Social Exclusion." *Science* 302, no. 5643 (October 10, 2003): 290–92. doi: 10.1126/science.1089134.

Mark, Gloria. "Multitasking in the Digital Age." *Synthesis Lectures on Human-Centered Informatics* (April 2015). doi.org/10.2200/S00635ED1V01Y201503HCI029.

Mehrabian, Albert and S.R. Ferris. "Inference of Attitudes from Nonverbal Communication in Two Channels." *Journal of Consulting Psychology* 31, no. 3 (1967): 248–252. doi.org/10.1037/h0024648.

Strochlic, Nina. "Why Do We Touch Strangers So Much? A History of the Handshake Offers Clues." *National Geographic*. March 16, 2020. NationalGeographic.co.uk /history-and-civilisation/2020/03/why-do-we-touch -strangers-so-much-history-of-handshake-offers.

Vaynerchuk, Gary. *Jab, Jab, Jab, Right Hook.* New York: HarperCollins, 2013.

Index

About the Author

Shola Kaye is an award-winning speaker and communication specialist. She's author of the book *How to Be a D.I.V.A. at Public Speaking*, creator of the podcast *Shortcuts to Public Speaking Success* (SholaKaye .com/podcast), and a TEDx speaker on empathy in the workplace. She's also a LinkedIn learning instructor with tens of thousands of students worldwide. Her work has been featured in *Harper's Bazaar* and *Marie Claire*.

As an introvert, Shola initially encountered her fair share of challenges related to speaking up and being heard. She now works in person and virtually with organizations worldwide to help them improve communication within their teams and boost diversity and inclusion, well-being, and leadership skills. Shola also coaches individuals who want to use speaking to promote their work, embark on a career as a professional speaker, or brush up on their day-to-day speaking skills.

Shola studied natural sciences at Cambridge University and then trained to be a teacher before getting a master's degree from Emory University. She can be found on LinkedIn (LinkedIn.com/in/sholakaye), Instagram (@speakuplikeadiva), and her website, SholaKaye.com.

CPSIA information can be obtained
at www.ICGtesting.com
Printed in the USA
BVHW090042301020
592002BV00003B/3